TINTINNABULATION OF LITERARY THEORY:

TRAVERSING GENRES TO CONTEMPORARY EXPERIENCE

Andrew Nyongesa

Mwanaka Media and Publishing Pvt Ltd,
Chitungwiza Zimbabwe
*
Creativity, Wisdom and Beauty

Publisher:
Mmap
Mwanaka Media and Publishing Pvt Ltd
24 Svosve Road, Zengeza 1
Chitungwiza Zimbabwe
mwanaka@yahoo.com
https//mwanakamediaandpublishing.weebly.com

Distributed in and outside N. America by African Books Collective
orders@africanbookscollective.com
www.africanbookscollective.com

ISBN: 978-0-7974-96439
EAN: 9780797496439

© Andrew Nyongesa 2018

All rights reserved.
No part of this book may be reproduced or transmitted in any form or by any means, mechanical or electronic, including photocopying and recording, or be stored in any information storage or retrieval system, without written permission from the publisher

DISCLAIMER
All views expressed in this publication are those of the author and do not necessarily reflect the views of *Mmap*.

ACKNOWLEDGEMENT

I wish to thank Dr. Murimi Gaita for his insightful lectures of theory in literature. I also appreciate Dr Wallace Mbugua for his emphasis on the importance of literary theory in literary criticism. I am indebted to Dr Justus Makokha for his wonderful exposition of feminism and exceptional mentorship. I will not forget Dr Kaigai Kimani for teaching me the nexus between postcolonial criticism and migration. Finally, I am grateful to Professor John Mugubi for his insightful exposition of stylistics and its essential role in literature.

Table of Contents

Introduction..v
Chapter 1: ASPECTS OF LITERARY THEORY 1
Chapter 2: MARXISTST THEORY 4
Chapter 3: FEMINIST THEORY..30
Chapter 4: POSTCOLONIAL CRITICISM............................59
Chapter 5: PSYCHOANALYTIC THEORY........................133
Chapter 6: STYSTICS- THE MAGIC WAND 172
Chapter 7: PHILOSOPHY AND CONTEMPORATY AFRICAN EXPERIENCE 200

Introduction

The recent past has seen the emergence of literary theory in literary criticism the world over. Literary critics in universities use philosophical ideas to analyse novels and plays to bolster knowledge of literature. Literary writers, particularly, novelists and playwrights base their works on philosophical canons that crown them great literatures. All these efforts are appreciable as they have drawn the study of literature away from the dreary of formalism where critics would only analyse plot, character, themes and style in a work of art. However, it is evident that the application of literary theory to oral literature (folklore) and contemporary African experiences is scarce.

In his essay, "What Philosophy can do Africa," Kwasi Wiredu observes that proponents of theory have ideas that can benefit the African continent and it is therefore imprudent to relegate philosophical ideas to the analysis of texts in journals. Besides applying theories on oral literature, the author in this book interrogates the benefits of philosophical ideas to the African society.

How best can Africa apply feminist ideas for her own good? How can Africa employ Bhabha's hybridity and Fanon's nationalism? If independent African leaders applied Fanon ideas, would Africa be as it is? Should politics be a preserve of political scientists when social scientists have mastery of the hearts and minds of the people? It is time to take literary theory away from the confines of the academic journal and apply it to day to day life like *Mwalimu* Julius Nyerere.

CHAPTER ONE:
ASPECTS OF LITERARY THEORY

Literary theory is the systematic study of literature; it is application of established canons like Marxism, post-colonialism, new historicism, psychoanalysis, travel theory, trauma theory and feminism to works of literature. Literary theory is a subset of literary criticism. Modern literary criticism is influenced by theory. Theory is concerned with the commonality between different proponents. All proponents of post colonialism for instance will focus on the struggle of the marginal group to upset the dominant group. From Edward Said, Frantz Fanon through to Homi Bhabha, they strive to destroy the narrative of the dominant group.

Theory has a number of aspects: first, it is speculative. The explanations that proponents of theory do offer cannot be verified to determine their truth or falsity. The feminists' claim that the position of women as endangered the world over cannot be attested to a few works of art from some communities because people are not homogeneous. There are many a community in the world with matriarchal systems and women lord it over men. Moreover, literary theory has a certain level of complexity that makes it tough to grasp. Jacquine Lacan's *The Mirror Stage* is a typical example of this. Lacan's infant (Cited from Rafey Habib), starts as something inseparable from its mother because it has no sense of self or individualized identity (7). When the baby looks at the mirror, it is able to recognize its image. It sees it as the ideal image; a complete form of the object (baby) and conceptualizes it as the other. The baby is now capable of distinguishing the *I* from the *other*, which is estrangement from oneself and the mother who is the Other. The child is now henceforth able to grow up as an independent subject. How will critic apply this complicated theory to literature? The intellectual complexity is quite evident.

Literary theory is multidisciplinary because most ideas stem from fields outside literature. Marxism emanates from the political and economic fields of knowledge; psychoanalysis is a branch of psychology, postcolonialism is quite political while feminism is both sociological and political.

Literary theory is practical. When literary critics and writers espouse theory, they think differently about issues that affect society. Theory brings common sense notions under detailed scrutiny. Under this aspect, we may define literary theory as a pugnacious critique of common sense notions. Michel Foucault, for instance, disputes definition of madness as violation of rationality or mental illness. Foucault observes that the European society imprisoned "poor vagabonds, criminals and the unemployed" (7) in the pretext that they were deranged minds. Anyone who behaved in manner that did not conform to the morals of society; anyone who looked miserable was undesirable and viewed as mad.

Moreover, literary theory is analytical as it breaks a concept clearly and highlights all its aspects. According to Sigmund Freud, writing is a mental illness which enables the writer to express his or her forbidden wishes. In his work *Interpretation of Dreams,* Freud observed that there is a tight relationship between the creative action and the artist and the neuroses and the role of the unconscious in the artistic creation must be determined. There is a close relationship between the artist and dreaming and for that reason, the artist is sort of mentally ill. Nawal El Saadawi's wicked desire to kill all oppressive men is concealed in Zakeya's decision to take a hoe and kill the Mayor in *God Dies by the Nile.* For Rousseau, writing gives the writer the ability to conceal the self or inner reality because the signs used by the writer are not transparent.

Literary theory is reflexive as it encourages critics to think deeply about subjects. Proponents of stylistics grapple with what really is literature as opposed to language. Wales K. (2001) defines stylistics as the study of literary style. He notes that the main aim of stylistics is not just description of the formal features of a text but "to show the functional significance for the interpretation of a text" (437). Wales therefore suggests that literary writers use style to express their subjects and themes. Literary language is therefore much different from language as it contains fragrant violation of linguistic norms. Literature is a speech act or textual event that elicits a certain kind of attention. It is aesthetic, and for Kant E. (1892), the aesthetic value has a purposiveness without a purpose," [12]. Kant possibly means that the end result of a work of art is nothing but art itself.

REFERENCES
Focault M. (1961). *Madness and Civilization.* London. Roultedge Classics.
Freud, S. (1900). *The Interpretation of Dreams.* London: Horgand.
Habib, M. (2008). *Modern Literacy Criticism and Theory: A History.* USA: Blackwell Publishing Ltd.
Wales, K (2001). *A Dictionary of Stylistics.* Harlow: Longman.
Kant E. (1951). *Crtitique of Judgement.* Trans. J. H Benard. New York. Hafner Publishing.

CHAPTER TWO:

MARXIST THEORY

2.1 Introduction

One of the oldest theories that have shaped the history of the world is Marxism. Many Western nations and world religions dreaded Marxism in the nineties, and the frosty relationships that exists between Russia and China on one hand and the West on the other stems from implementation of Marxism in former nations. Marxism challenged religion and existing political systems thereby causing world tensions. Historians believe that the failure of Britain and France to stop the rise of Nazzism was deliberate because they saw Hitler as a solution to Marxism. France and Britain wanted Adolf Hitler to destroy Russia and eradicate communism. Walsh B. (2008) writes:

> Stalin had been very worried about the German threat to Soviet Union ever since Hitler came to power in 1933. Hitler had openly stated his interest in conquering Russian land. He had denounced communism and imprisoned and killed communists in Germany. Even so, Stalin could not reach any kind of lasting agreement with Britain and France.[...] indeed some in Britain seemed even to welcome a stronger Germany as a force to fight communism. (271)

These are Stalin's suspicions that laid the foundation to the Cold War after 1945. For Marx, Communism is the praxis of socialism where a classless society is formed after a socialist revolution. Although Marx observed that communism is the end-product of spontaneous evolution in society, Lenin insisted that communism has to be imposed on society. In November 1917, Lenin overthrew the Kerensky capitalist Russian regime and imposed communism (Walsh, 114). He established what he called "a dictatorship of the proletariat".

Lois Tyson observes that Marxist criticism looks at the relationship among socio-economic classes within and among societies and explains human activities in dynamics of economic power. Tyson asserts that "the theory holds that getting and keeping economic power is the motive behind all social and political activities including education, philosophy, religion, government, arts, science, technology and media" (54). She states other tenets as follows:

First, differences in socioeconomic class divide people in ways that are more significant than differences in religion, race ethnicity and gender. For Max, real battle lines are drawn between the rich and the poor rather than basic diversities like sex, race, ethnicity and religion. Secondly, the proletariat (peasants and poor workers) will one day spontaneously develop the class consciousness needed to rise up in violent revolution against their oppressors and create a classless society. This is the socialist revolution, the ultimate goal of socialism that is geared at creating a classless society. Thirdly, ideology is an essential feature of the Marxist theory. Ideology refers to the belief systems of a people such as religion or political philosophies like democracy, aristocracy, autocracy and economic beliefs like capitalism and communism. These ideologies have a role of maintaining those in power. Religion, according to Marx, helps to keep the laity poor and satisfied with their lot in life.

2:2 Marxism Vis-a-Vis the Novel and the Play

As the latest genre of literature, literary writers in Africa and beyond used the novel to convey the need to create a Marxist society. Drama was not left behind; playwrights wrote plays and had them directed and staged to sell Marxist ideals. Between 1945 and 1990, the cutthroat competition between Marxism and capitalism infiltrated works of fiction to persuade audiences towards their sides. In East Africa, Mwalimu Julius Nyerere fell for Marxist ideals and translated Shakespeare's *The Marchant of Venice* to the socialist Swahili version: *Mapepari wa Venisi* (The capitalists of Venice). Ngugi wa Thiong'o in Kenya opted for Marxism and based most of his plays and novels on the canon. *I will Marry when I Want* for instance exhibits a class struggle in which the factory owners are portrayed as blood suckers who exploit the poor workers. In *A Grain of Wheat*, there is a class struggle between the poor freedom fighters on one hand and the bourgeoisie colonialists with their obsequious home guards. Mugo's betrayal suggests that the independent leaders were mistakenly given the instruments of power because they were the very people who worked in cahoots with the imperial capitalists to exploit the workers. In *Petals of Blood*, Ngugi hails the role of workers in bringing real change in Kenya. He decries tribal divisions sown by the independence government and insists that the only tribes in existence are the rich and the poor. He interrogates the logic behind thieves who steal and when other leaders question them, they incite their ethnic communities that other communities want to reap where they did not sow. As the story comes to a close, the workers are going to the forest to fight for independence afresh. After publication of *Petals of Blood*, Ngugi was detained owing to its Marxist ideals that attacked the capitalistic Kenyan regime. In *The Devil on the Cross*, Ngugi depicts Marxist ideals by portraying Kenyan capitalist leaders as thieves who wait after the workers have crucified the colonialist on the cross and they sneak there to resurrect him. No Novelist in East Africa employed the Marxist canon in the novel better than Ngugi wa Thiong'o. His caricature of religion, attack on the rich factory owners and the capitalist ideology is enormous. In North Africa, Nawal El Saadawi's novels depict a class struggle as we shall elaborate in the next subsections. Although she majorly is a proponent of the feminist canon, her experiences under colonialism, Nasser administration and many others have influenced her and sometimes uses Marxism to attack oppressive capitalism. Let us now analyse Marxism in the novel.

2:2.1 Class and Political Stability: A Marxist Study of Nawal El Saadawi's *God Dies by the Nile* and Safi Abdi's *Offspring of Paradise*.

Nawal El Saadawi's *God Dies by the Nile* and Safi Abdi's *Offspring of Paradise* explore the impact of social class on political stability of the society. Acute class differences underscore conflict between the rich and poor, which destabilize the nation. The conflict is imperiled by the rich class lording it over the poor to provoke a violent reaction from the poor classes, a reaction whose consequences tatter the social fabric and destroys a nation. The ruling classes in the Horn of Africa nation- Somalia relegate the poor clans, which rise up against the regime in Abdi's *Offspring of Paradise*. Siyad Barre, the Somalia despotic leader favours his Marehan clan with high profile jobs in government and disregards other clans. Hana, Abdi's heroine hails from the ruling clan and hence suffers as victim of the socialist revolution. So does the mayor oppress and commit despicable acts against the villagers in Kafr El Teen. The peasant, Zakeya, for instance represents the proletariat who rise against the bourgeoisie's economic and sexual exploitation in Saadawi's *God Dies by the Nile*.

2:2.2 Marxist Critique of *God Dies by the Nile*

Set in beautiful sleepy village, Kafr El Teen, El Saadawi's *God Dies by the Nile* is about the avaricious rich class embodied in a corrupt, tyrannical mayor. Embraced by the king and the British imperialists, he takes advantage of his position to detain peasant men and exploit their women sexually. The story begins with Zakeya, the heroine, digging on the farm, with a buffalo beside her. Kaffrawi, her brother, comes to report that his daughter, Naffissa has disappeared from the village. From the outset, we suspect the mayor's role in the disappearance. He is described as having "[h]aughty eyes, almost arrogant quality like those of an English gentleman, accustomed to command," (10). The mayor's arrogance that stems from his bourgeoisie class has contributed to exploitation and oppression of many poor people in Kafr El Teen, for example the detention of Galal, Zakeya's son who marries Zeinab, the death of Elwau, Naffissa's husband and Zakeya's niece, the death of Fatheya, the beautiful woman who marries Sheikh Hamzawi and detention of Kaffrawi, Zakeya's brother. These unbecoming acts infuriate Zakeya who resolves to kill the mayor to end the suffering of the poor at Kafr El Teen. He is the "God" referred to in the title of the novel since he has taken God's place by determining the life span of the people. He is sovereign, he kills those he wants and spares those that he wants. He appoints and demotes the clerics and so they must all kowtow before him.

El Saadawi's *God Dies by the Nile* subscribes to the tenets of Marxist criticism. The story for instance proves that the economic power determines the superstructure since most of the characters are motivated by obtaining material power in every endeavor they undertake. The mayor of Kafr El Teen is so greedy that he has used peasant's taxes to live lavishly. In the preface of the book, El Saadawi writes, "[t]he mayor exploited peasants to serve the king's interests and the king exploited peasants to serve the interests of the British army in the Suez," (vii). The mayor's elder brother went to school to obtain intellectual and economic power. He is so rich and influential politician that whenever he appears on the headlines of the newspaper, the mayor suffers psychosomatic fits of jealousy. Most of the religious activities by characters in the story have monetary intentions. The holy sheikhs at El Sayeda Mosque "heals people at a fee of ten pastries" (112). Zakeya complains that "even God wants to be paid something yet He knows that the poor have nothing" (100). The other religious leaders like Sheikh Hamzawi preach for a wage and he has to kowtow and bless the Mayor to protect his source of income. When the Mayor turns against Hamzawi, he is assaulted and demoted from his responsibility.

The story depicts the relationship between the haves and the have nots. The King, the British and the mayor belong to the ruling bourgeoisie that controls the means of production. Zakeya, Kaffrawi, Galal, Hamzawi, Hajj Ismail are the peasants or proletariat who pulsate under the former's avarice. The mayor takes advantage of his position to exploit peasant women. The women represent the society of Kafr El Teen, which is abused by the ruling elite. In his solitary moments, he says, "[h]ow exciting these simple (peasant) girls are, how pleasant it is to take their virgin bodies into one's arms," (120). When Galal, Zakeya's son loves Zeinab, the girl that the mayor has designs on; Galal is charged with failure to pay taxes and imprisoned. The bourgeoisie therefore take advantage of their power to exploit and frustrate the peasants.

El Saadawi further proves that differences in socioeconomic class divide characters more than differences in religion, ethnicity and race. The mayor of Kafr El Teen boasts of having descended from the white race because his father married a white woman given his high class. He identifies himself with the king and the British. He tells the villagers, "[c]ompared to me you people are just nobodies, the way peasants take *shebet* is the way the rich take milk" (15). That is why he kills Elwau and Fatheya even if they too are Muslims. They belong to the poor class, which he despises and looks down on. Frustrated by the mayor's contempt and maltreatment of the poor: the murder of Elwau, detention of her son Galal, the demotion and assault of sheikh Hamzawi and the lynching of Fatheya, Zakeya takes the peasants cause in her hands and murders the Mayor- the 'God' of Kafr El Teen. This is a Marxist revolution after the peasants gaining consciousness. Zakeya symbolizes this consciousness; she is fed up by the bourgeoisie's acts of avarice. Her mental illness is as a result of economic and social problems rooted in the capitalism ideology. It works through a deceptive religion that pacifies and exploits the peasantry. The Sheikh's therapy, for instance prescribes sexual exploitation of Zeinab and imprisonment of Galal. The man who plays God calls Zakeya at El Sayeda Mosque and says that Zakeya's sickness is caused by disobedience and prescribes a solution, "Zeinab is to walk towards the iron gate, open it and walk in and should not walk out of it again until the owner of the house orders him to do so," (115). The religion prescribes Zeinab having sex with the mayor as a cure of Zakeya's psychological sickness, which she does without any sign of healing. That is why the mayor imprisons Galal, Zeinab's fiancé, out of jealousy.

Ideology therefore plays a crucial role in maintaining the position of the bourgeoisie in power. Those with psychological problems stemming from poverty are directed to seek solutions in religion. Sheikh Hajj Ismail directs Zeinab to have sex with the mayor to get a solution to his problems as a sign of submission to the ruling elite. In his preaching, Sheikh Hamzawi takes time to bless the mayor: "[t]hat Allah may bestow long life to the mayor- the best mayor we have ever had in Kafr El Teen, he always seeks truth and justice" (135).

God Dies by the Nile does not reinforce capitalist values; the writer is so bitter with domination of the peasantry by the bourgeoisie. She critiques capitalism and imperialism for institutionalizing religion to exploit and oppress the poor. El Saadawi critiques organized religion because it pacifies the peasant women to remain subject to exploitation of the rich. The novel is ideologically conflicted as it supports Marxism in capitalistic system. It further reflects socioeconomic conditions in which it was written; it is set in Egypt at the onset of colonial rule when the Khedive Ismail (the king) ruled in conjunction with British imperialist to exploit peasant Egyptians.

2:2.3 Marxist Critique of Safi Abdi's *Offspring of Paradise*

According to the Marxist theory, literature is a reflection of the unending, irreconcilable class struggle between the ruling class and the proletariat in the society or the working class' dream of a way out of oppression or dream of realizing their utopia. In Abdi's *Offspring of Paradise,* the ruling class, Mohamed Siyad Barre with his cronies, enrich their clan and subjugate other clans. The proletariat represented by the militia group start guerrilla warfare against the government that spreads from Mogadishu to many parts of Somalia. By 1991, they have overwhelmed government resistance and overthrow Barre regime. They victimize the ruling clan, brand it *fagash*-loyalists and embark on ethnic cleansing to realize their utopian dream of equality. They occupy *fagash's* homes and murder them. Mulki, who hails from the militia clan, is compelled to disown her friend Zahra, "[y]ou are *faqash,* your home is not your home" (19). Hana, who hails from the ruling clan loses her father in a grenade attack, her mother is almost burnt and loses her memory.

Offspring of Paradise begins when a military junta overthrows the government of Somalia and assumes the reins. The new military leader who hails from the Marehan clan preserves high profile jobs for his clansmen. The heroine, Hana, hails from this clan and that is why his father and uncle are high ranking officials in government. One of her relatives, Zahra, is a student at a national university when the government is overthrown. Another of her relatives, Amina has a husband with postgraduate qualifications and owns a spacious house in Magadishu. Zahra and her friend, Mulki, go to university to increase their chances of gaining economic power. When Mulki becomes a refugee in a Western country, she gets a job as an interpreter due to her higher education and becomes economically stable. Rune, Jason and Helen work for the refugee camp in the white country to gain economic power. Most of the characters in the novel pursue politics, religion and education to gain economic power.

The novel portrays the tense and hostile relationship between different classes in Somalia. The ruling clan- Marehan favours its own with opportunities and grows richer than other clans like Majeertan and Isaaq. Historian Joakim Gundel observes that Siyad Barre denied these clans water and many died of thirst. They therefore form a militia group that overthrows the regime and persecutes the ruling clan. They label the ruling clan *fagash-* loyalists and murder thousands of them. Hana's father is assassinated and the mother escapes with a horrible burn on her face.

It is evident that differences in socioeconomic class divide people more than differences in religion and ethnicity. In spite of Somalis professing same religion and hailing from same ethnic group, real battle lines are drawn along class. The Siyad Barre regime causes class differences by favoring one clan with economic opportunities, water and education. As a result, religion is shoved aside and a socialist revolution commences. At the beginning of the story, Zakariya tells Ahmed that he cannot rob him because they profess same religion. Ahmed retorts, "[d]on't Zakariya me, be gone, fagash," (5). The militia groups, who have been impoverished by the exploitation of the ruling class, turn the apple cart: they comb out Marehan by interrogating them for family lineage and executing them. She writes:

> Who is this?
> Utiya…the great granddaughter of so and so
> So and so… who?
> The so and so who died and left behind only Utiya's grandfather
> So and so…remember that great uncle of ours? The one who married into so
> And so branch of the tribe. Which branch of tribe? (23)

Zahra's attempt to hide at Mulki's family comes to a futile end. Mulki's brothers refuse to protect her and Mulki's father hides her in a bush where he is eaten by wild game. Mulki's father reprimands his son Abdullahi for refusing to protect Zahra but the son shoots his father just to show the perilous degree to which the revolution has reached.

Religion as the ideology in *Offspring of Paradise* fails to keep the ruling class in power. The dictator's attempt to create a personality cult fails when the proletariat defies the demands of the religion and fight back. Abdi writes: "[n]ow what did you do about spilling of Muslim blood? Is this piece of flesh more sacred? Muslims killing Muslims?" (72).

Unlike El Saadawi who rejects imperialism and capitalism, Abdi supports them. She is uncomfortable with the revolution because she says that Somalia was better than it is now. She writes, "[t]his government was all about force and coercion yet it had the knack to keep all pieces in place" (19). The novel reflects the socioeconomic conditions in which it was written. Siyad Barre was deposed in 1991 and most members of his clan were persecuted and fled from Somalia to all parts of the world. The "death of Khalif, Hana's maternal uncle in Buro" (87), refers to the struggle of Somali Salvation Democratic Front led by Abdullahi Yusuf Ahmed and members of the Isaaq clan against government forces. Joakim Gundel observes that the Barre regime made many raids in the north to quell these groups (263). Although the author suggests that most people benefited from the regime,, the regime isolated three clans: Majeerten, Hawiye and Isaaq. The Red Berets, Barre's secret terrorists, smashed water points to deny them water. More than two thousand members died of thirst and five thousand killed by Red Beret. The novel critiques organized religion as the writer seems to wonder why it cannot hold people together.

2.3 Marxist Critique of African Poetry

Song of the worker
Songonyi

We squat
We move
Left centre right
Breaking stones
Kwa! Kwa! Kwa!

Our hands sore
Our heads ache
Our knees numb
Our backs break
Breaking stones
Kwa! Kwa! Kwa!

> We squat
> We move
> Back centre forward
> Tilling the land
> Kwa! Kwa! Kwa!
>
> Our song is sorrow
> Our tears we eat
> In rags we move
> Tramping the land
> Kwa! Kwa! Kwa!
> To them it is dance
> They roar in laughter
> While we sweat and bleed
>
> To them
> it's pleasure
> they weep with laughter
> while we stumble and tumble
> Burdened and hungry
> Kwa! Kwa! Kwa! Kwa! Kwa! (Amateshe, 1989, P. 34)

In this poem, Songonyi presents two classes of people in this society that are quite conscious of their class differences. We have the proletariat or poor workers represented by quarry workers who break stones. The idiophonic words *kwa kwa kwa* express the toil they go through to get their daily bread. The hard physical work gives them headaches and sores their hands (our hands sore). The hard work embitters them (in tears we eat) and they cannot afford to buy fine clothes. For Marx, anything human beings apply themselves on, they have economic interests. In the poem all human activity is geared towards attaining material rewards. The quarry workers sweat as they labour to be paid for the survival of their families.

The workers are very conscious of another class of people in the society who avariciously use them for their vanities. The persona says, "[t]o them/ it's dance," (line 22/23). The *them* are the selfish, exploitative landowners or bourgeoisie who share out the profits made by workers among themselves. For Marx, the class consciousness degenerates gradually to violent revolution. The persona is whipping up workers emotion to heed the call to a socialist revolution that would establish a communist state- a classless society.There is the assumption among the workers that their problem emanates from the exploitation by the wealthy class and that is why the persona is more embittered by their laughter. When the rich enjoy themselves, the workers believe it is their sweat they are expending; for Marx, profit is the sweat of the workers, which should be shared equally among the proletariat. Let us analyse another poem:

The Dog in Kivulu
Ralph Bitamazire

The dog in Kivulu
Thin, bony and yawning;
The dog in Kivulu
Panting and squatting
Like its master.
The dog in Kivulu,
Barking at naked children,
Children who sing a thanksgiving
As they leave the rubbish heaps.
The dog in Kivulu
Running away from fat flies

> And scratching its tail with teeth,
> Biting nothing but its own gums
> Swallowing nothing more than its own saliva.
> The dog of Kivulu,
> Guarding its drunkard master
> And the hoard of fermenting millet…
> But the dog of Kivulu lies by with nothing to drink;
> Nobody calls it Acaali, the bitch,
> It looks on- at the trenches-
> And drinks the water from the cattle shed (Cook & Rubadiri, 1971, p. 22)

Bitamazire's "The Dog in Kivulu" presents class differences in a slum called Kivulu in Kampala, Uganda. The rich class exploit or abuse the poor class by low pay and ill-treatment such that their life is beastly. The squalor in which the poor live has reduced them into animals. A first glance at the poem gives the suggestion that the persona is talking about a dog living in Kivulu. A critical look at the poem reveals that the persona is talking about a worker, possibly a janitor who guards a rich master who deals in production and sale of cheap liquor. The persona says, "The dog of Kivulu/ Guarding its drunkard master/And the hoard of fermenting millet," to prove that the dog is a human being. His harrowing experiences of abject poverty and oppression by the landowners have dehumanized him so much that he behaves like an animal. He is savage or violent and cannot speak politely. He "barks at naked children" instead of being courteous to them. These are the street urchins, which is another element of the poor class in Kivulu. They search for food in the rubbish heaps as the janitor bites nothing but his gums for food. He also drinks water from the trenches. There is a brewing class conflict on this part of Kampala because the janitor "flees fat flies" to signify hatred between him and the rich class. The title, "Dog in Kivulu" suggests a spiteful attitude of the rich towards the poor; there is no iota of sympathy among the haves towards the have nots. The persona possibly belongs to the high class, which criminalizes the poor and relegates them to the non-human. This poem gives a clear reflection of most slums in Africa where class conflicts instigate crimes such as robbery and violence as the poor strive to close the economic gap between the rich and the poor. For Marxism a robber plays a crucial role in balancing the wealth between the rich and the poor. Let us analyse another poem under Marxist theory:

The Guilt of Giving
Laban Erapu

You"ve seen that heap of rags
That pollutes the air conditioned
City centre,
That louse that creeps about
In the clean core of sophistication;
You've seen him waylay his betters
And make them start-
Especially when they have no change.

You recall the day you came upon him
And were startled by his silence presence
Intruding into your preoccupation:
You hurled a coin
Which missed the mark
And rolled into the gutter
Where he groped for it
With a chilling grotesque gratitude

> That followed you down the street.
> You dived into a nearest shop
> To escape the stare
> Of the scandalized crowd
> That found you guilty
> Of recalling attention
> To the impenetrable patience
> They had learnt not to see. (Cook &Rubadiri, 1971, p. 42)

Laban Erapu in this poem delves into the class differences and brings his poem under Marxist Criticism. The juxtaposition of the beggar and the air conditioned city centre suggests how a few have taken advantage of their positions to own tall, sophisticated property in cities while the majority languishes in poverty. The beggar represents the poorest of the poor in urban centres who look at people for assistance. The rich who are supposed to assist the poor are guilty of their avarice, which creates a class conflict at the City Centre. The rich man "hurls a coin" and it misses the beggar and he crawls into the gutter to take it. For Marx, the two classes get conscious of their class and it gradually builds up to a conflict. The rich man is aware of his high class and the avarice he has used to acquire his wealth. This explains the violence he metes out on the beggar via throwing of the coin. "The Guilt of Giving" is a true reflection of class differences in urban centres in Africa today where robbery gangs spontaneously emerge to close the gap between the rich and the poor. For Marx, the robber plays the essential role of balancing wealth between the bourgeoisie and proletariat. The crowd is scandalized not because of the rich man's insolent act, but his attempt to remind them that the beggar is supposed to be assisted. They are so dehumanized by capitalistic greed that they cannot assist anyone. Here the mantra is, "[m]an for himself, God for us all."

2.4 Marxist Critique of Oral Literature

The following oral narrative was collected from the Bukusu community of Western Kenya, but is collected and written in Nyongesa A. (2017). Let us attempt a Marxist critique of the narrative:

"Long time ago, there lived an old woman whom Wele had given an only son called Ngiti", she began.

The old woman was very poor but Wele Khakaba had given her the skill of weaving and knitting. The old woman happened to have a wound on the shin, the kind that never harkened to cure. Mother and son led a life of luxury in *Mwitukhu* above the sky. They never touched a hoe; they never toiled with livestock for their living. They idled their time away in all sorts of pleasures as people down on earth toiled with their hoes to plant; to weed, to prune.

They watched and laughed as Ngiti wove a rope. The old woman would look at her wound exulting in it, not wishing its recovery. At harvest time, she would strut across the lash home and gaze at people on earth. She could see some stranded with the bounty harvest. That was her joy.

Ngiti would then unroll the long rope and gripping it tightly, she would dangle down to earth to assist the farmers. She would accost them to strike a bargain.

"Are you desperate?" she would ask.

"For?"

"Transport".

"Yes, grandee, may Wele help us".

"In fact He's with you this morning. He 'll never take His eye away from his righteous".

"That's true".

"Pack all this harvest into my wound and all will be well with you".

"Stop your jokes ma", they laughed doubtfully.

"Doubt spoiled a blessing, my children, just believe".

"All this harvest can't ..."

"The sage cautioned against too many questions. Just be silent, don't ask many questions."

The farmers would obey her. They would thrust their harvest into the wound and truly, her shin would guzzle it all. The grandee would then sing a song in the language of the skies, which the farmer admired but understood not.

Khakele khange, Ngiti	*My good shin, Ngiti*
Khakhila omulimi, Ngiti	*is better than a farmer, Ngiti*
Khakhila omwaki, Ngiti	*is better than a tiller, Ngiti*
Ngiti, Ngiti, Ngiti	*Ngiti, Ngiti, Ngiti*
Omwana wanje, Ngiti	*My son, Ngiti*
Ikhisia omukoye, Ngiti	*Unroll the rope, Ngiti*
Ikhisia omukoye, Ngiti	*Unroll the rope, Ngiti*
Ngiti, Ngiti, Ngiti	*Ngiti, Ngiti, Ngiti.*

Ngiti would hear the demanding tone of his mother's voice and send the rope dangling down to earth. His mother would grasp it tautly and he would pull her up to their luxurious mansion in heavens. The farmers could gawk at their annual produce receding into the heavens quick and fast. They would call obscenities; they would leap in disgust and stamp on the ground. They would swear by earth and tear their outfit but the truth was that the fruit of their perspiration was gone with the mysterious rope and wound.

The following season, she would go to another village; and that was their life.

(Adapted from Andrew Nyongesa's The Blissabyss).

The above oral narrative from the Bukusu community in Kenya has features that bring it under Marxist Criticism. There are two classes of people, the rich class: Ngiti and his mother who have the means to live in an ivory tower, far above the common workers such as farmers, blacksmiths, hunters and others. Ngiti and the mother are so rich that they are said to live in the sky. The wound in the story represents inability to do menial jobs, but are endowed with intellectual or business acumen, which they take advantage of to exploit the poor. Ngiti and his mother are possibly business people who have exploited workers and made billions thereby living luxurious lives in cities. The rope represents money, machines and other lofty high tech devices they own such as lorries, trains, airplanes. The farmers work many months, but when harvest time comes, the avaricious businessmen use the law of demand and supply to lower the prices of produce and ferry it at a throw away price to their warehouses in urban centres. They store the produce to wait for hard times and sell at high prices to make billions. The narrator is therefore a capitalist who brags that his or her business acumen is far better than sheer hard work on the farm, blacksmithing, masonry and carpentry. He sneers at trades practiced by the poor class and lauds skills mastered by doctors, engineers, the chief executives, lawyers and the academia, which bring in more income without physical labours. The farmers are conscious of the class differences and call obscenities to lay a foundation for the impending class conflict. For Marx, the two classes get conscious of their class differences and it culminates into a physical conflict referred to as a socialist revolution. Ngiti and his mother may not survive the next time.

In the next section we shall analyse some African proverbs under the Marxist canon:

First is the proverb, "The neck is not measured by the arm" (Miruka, 50). It means all men are not granted things equally and therefore gives a hint into the class differences. The Bukusu community from which the proverb is derived acknowledges the existence of the rich land owners and the poor workers. The speaker of this proverb uses it in self defense because the rich class are possibly compelling him or her to give more than they can afford. The proverb therefore justifies the workers' poverty for psychological relief.

Second is the Luo proverb, " Hallo, don't let one herd cross the path of the other," which means a father should look after the children just the way he looks after his cattle. The proverb places both children and cattle under the category of wealth or the material hence echoing Marx's claim that the economic base determines the consciousness. Whether humankind ventures in the religious, seeks political power or pursues family life, for Marx, they want material rewards. The above proverb suggests that people start family to seek material gain just as cattle is reared for that purpose. Just as the attention that is given to cattle has vested interests so does parenting. Many Africans will candidly assert that they look after the girl child in the hope that she will get married to a man who will pay dowry, which is economic gain. Feminist critics have in recent past questioned the ethical value of dowry in African societies and literary writer like Margaeret Ogola portrays it as an immoral act of selling the girl to slavery.

Third is the Swahili proverb, *Mweye Njaa hana miiko*, which means a hungry person does not observe taboos. Poverty will provoke someone to flout conventions to earn his or her daily bread. One can steal, rob and fight to survive. For Marx, the poor has nothing to lose but the whole world to gain, and so their poverty compels them to defy conventions by stealing and robbing the rich. The probability of the poor being involved in violent revolution is higher than that of the bourgeoisie because they have no material wealth to protect. Taboos, rules and laws, according to Marxism are instruments of the rich to exploit the poor, and that is why they have chosen a state of anarchy to overthrow the dominant landowners.

Fourth is the Luo proverb, *Dher ariemba wuongo nyiedho to ng'iyo oko* translated as the custodian of a loaned cow milks it while looking out (Miruka, 79). Class differences are evident in the proverb because the giver of the loan is a rich bourgeoisie, but the indebted person is a proletariat who uses collateral to secure the loan. The loan is therefore not theirs and has to spend it carefully. In the event of failure to pay, the loan giver will take the little the loanee has or even use the law to jail. There is already a class conflict because of deep seated anxiety between the rich giver and the recipient. The rich man is only at peace when he has the assurance that the poor worker is paying the loan. The worker uses the loan with the fear that the rich man will not change his mind and ask for his money. Anything can happen to trigger the class conflict between the two and the rich merchant will use the law as the peasant resorts to the use of the robbers to break into the bank.

Finally is the proverb, "It is from where you work that you eat," (Miruka, 84) which means that a person derives his livelihood from where he or she works. The proverb is in tandem with Marxist tenet that the economic base determines the consciousness. The material gain dominates the human desire to pursue everything in the social, political and economic spheres. Work, in this community's view is for material benefit. It gives us access to the means that provide for our food, shelter, clothing and luxuries like cars, cosmetics and jewellery. Work is not meant for abstract gains like fame and self expression, but provision of the daily bread and we should take it seriously.

2.5 Marxism and Drama

As earlier mentioned, drama has been a vehicle that conveyed Marxism the world over. Communists used theatre as a means of selling the Marxism to their audiences. The United States of America, the leader of capitalists during the Cold War, censored such works of fiction. The prologue of Bretchet's *Caucasian Chalk Circle* was not permitted on stage in the United States. In this section, we shall do a Marxist analysis of one play by the German playwright Bertolt Bretchet.

2:5.1 The *Caucasian Chalk Circle,* a Marxist Propaganda

"Who is a true mother to a child? Is it the biological mother or she that brings it up?" this is the pertinent question by many a critic wherever Bretchet's *Caucasian Chalk Circle* is studied. The perspective stems from deliberate negation of the prologue, which is the play itself. The dispute between the two communes: Rosa Luxenburg, the goat keepers and Galinsk, the fruit growers over the valley and its resolution by the commissioner from Tiflis presents the major conflict and subject of the play. The rest of events from "Noble Child" to the "Chalk Circle" are a song that is performed by a singer Arkadi Tcheidse to grace the occasion. It is absurd for readers to forget the main issues (Marxist land tenets) and focus on the minor event, which is just an analogy to reinforce the subject in the prologue. Brechet's *Caucasian Chalk Circle* is not a story on motherhood but a propaganda piece that inculcates Marxist ideals.

The play upholds the materialism tenet of the Marxist philosophy. According to Karl Marx, the economic base determines the superstructure. Every human activity aims at economic benefits. Land should therefore be owned by people who will utilize it for economic production but not to those who claim to be aborigines of the place. Galinski Commune have a plan to use the land for the economic benefit of the populace: they plan to construct a dam and irrigate 700 hactres to grow vineyards (P. 10). Rosa Luxemburg's major claim is that the valley is their ancestral land. The air smells better and the bread tastes better at the valley. The Marxist commissioner dismisses Rosa's defense as sham and hands the valley to Galinski Commune. As much as Rosa Luxemburg's reasons are dismissed on the grounds of fairness, Bretchet devalues the conventional concept of ancestral land. He seems to imply that it is capitalistic and unfairly rewards lazy communities at the expense of diligent ones who can better utilize land for the common good. But is this not justification of forceful eviction of people from their ancestral lands in the pretext that they have no use for it? Josef Stalin evicted millions of Russians from their ancestral lands basing on this tenet.

Besides the belief in materialism, Bretchet presents the Marxist notion of class and ideology. For Marx class consciousness supersedes ethnic and racial leanings and so Bretchet chooses characters to depict class conflict. The bourgeoisie class comprises the Grand Duke, the princes, Georgi Abashwili and his wife Natella. They posses land, labour and capital as the poor workers such as the petitioners and beggars languish in poverty. Georgi Abashwili is affluent and owns horses, servants, a beautiful wife and a baby. Natella, his snobbish wife, is a palpable symbol of the governor's status. In court, she underscores the class divide when she blurts that the poor have an odour that causes her migraine (P. 88). The playwright depicts the Marxist belief that the Christian religion cements the class divide by showing the rich first family marching to church for the Easter Sunday service surrounded by poor beggars and petitioners. One pleads for the release of his only son from the army while another one complains about the corrupt water inspector. The governor directs the adjutant to chase the petitioners away with a whip (p.14). Bretchet's juxtaposition of the governor's lavish lifestyle with the poor subjects at the gate is a depiction class differences and conflict as a Marxist tenet. The playwright implies that the difference between classes proceeds to the summit, which is a socialist revolution. And this happens when Georgi Abashwili is overthrown and beheaded (p. 20). Marxism is therefore explicitly depicted in the play.

Azdak, the judge of the poor man embodies communist perspectives about the law and leadership. From the outset, Azdak (a former rabbit thief) amazes the iron shirts with his knowledge and they elect him the chief justice. Soon after he becomes judge, Azdak places the Statute Book on the chair and sits on it. He therefore presides over cases by determining the class of the person to favour them if poor and exploit them if rich. He takes bribes from the rich and punishes them; he is gentle to the poor and acquits them; for example the case of Ludovica and the stableman. Though it is a case of rape, the poor stableman is acquitted and Lodovica, the victim is fined (p.78). Bretchet depicts a number of Marxist ideals in the character of Azdak: a petty thief is not a criminal; he is better than a police officer (Shauwa) who steals from poor people. A petty thief can therefore be a leader. Azdak's sitting on a Statute Book signifies the communist view that the law is the instrument of the rich to exploit the poor. The ruling elite steal from the poor worker via the fines levied in court.

Finally, Azdak's treatment of the robber Irakli embodies Marxist ideals. Irakli is a robber and witch mistakenly referred to as Saint Banditus by the peasants. He steals a cow from a rich farmer and gives it to an old woman who lost her son during the war. The farmer sues the old woman and Irakli appears in court as a witness with an axe (p.80). Unexpectedly, Azdak welcomes the robber warmly and lets him be served with a drink of vodka. He recites some lines to express his sympathy for the old woman (Granny of Grusinia). The verdict of the case is shocking: the old woman and Irakli are acquitted but the farmers, fined five hundred piasters (p.82). The case embodies a queer Marxist ideal appertaining to robbery and class struggle. For Marxism, a robber belongs to the proletariat class who plays the role of distributing the wealth between the rich and the poor; hence the work of Irakli.

It is apparent that the obsession with motherhood as the subject of Bretchet's *Caucasian Chalk Circle* is beside the point. Motherhood is a shroud that prevents the audience to understand the crude Marxist ideals behind it. Accurate criticism will break the shroud to bring the audience to the knowledge that the two mothers: Natella and Grusha are metaphors. Natella represents capitalists who believe in spiritual connection to ancestral lands but Grusha is the communist who believes in productive use of land. Eviction of people from their ancestral land under the pretext that they have no use for it is callous and illegal. It is not therefore surprising that the prologue of the play was not performed in the United States of America; the Marxism in it is intoxicating.

2:6 Conclusion

In this chapter, we have analysed diverse genres of literature by use of Marxist Criticism. The chapter begun by outlining the tenets of Marxist theory and proceeded by traversing the different literary genres in search for them. It is evident that the novel, drama, poetry and genres of African folklore portray the Marxist canon.

REFERENCES

Abdi, S. (2004).*Offspring of Paradise*. Bloomington: Authorhouse.
Amateshe A. (1989). Introduction to East African Poetry. Nairobi. EAEP
Bretch, B. (1948). *The Caucasian Chalk Circle*. Nairobi.Target Publication Ltd.
Cook, D. & Rubadiri, D. (1971). *Poems from East Africa*. Nairobi. EAEP.
Gundel, J. (2001)*The Migration Development Nexus- Somalia Case Study*. Copenhagen:
Blackwell Publishers.
Marx, K. (1859).*A Contribution to Critique of Political Economy*. Moscow. Progress Publishers.
Miruka, O. (1994). *Encounter with Oral Literature*.Nairobi. EAEP.
Nyongesa, A. (2017). The Blissabyss. Mauritius. JustFiction.
Saadawi, E. N. (1974).*God Dies by the Nile*. London. Zed Books.
Tyson, L. (2006). *Critical Theory Today*.New York. Routledge.
Walsh, B. (1996).GCSE *Modern World History*. London: Hodder Murray.

CHAPTER THREE:

THE FEMINIST THEORY

3:1 Introduction

A week hardly comes to a close without a headline on the need to protect the girl child and the woman from oppression by men. So and so has taken advantage of his position to abuse women sexually or male teachers who talk to girls more often should be sacked are common items of news in our world. Governments strive to make laws that try to improve the position of the woman to demystify male domination. In the 90s, novelists could not publish in Kenya without female characters that outshine men. In universities, many lecturers taught lesssons that potrayed the woman as a victim and loser of the gender war and many male sudents were either disheartened or joined the bandwagon to become feminists. As a result, there is a surge in single women albeit with stunning achievements in life. In Kenya, there are many male children with female surnames: Philip Sarah, Elizabeth Mumbi and Simon Eunice owing to the women rights movements.

Lois Tyson defines feminist criticism as a theory that examines ways in which literature reinforces or undermines the economic, political, social and psychological oppression of women (83-92). She comes up with other tenets of the theory: women are oppressed by patriarchy economically, socially, politically and psychologically; in every domain where patriarchy reigns, the woman is the *other;* she is marginalized. All of Western civilization is deeply rooted in patriarchy; while biology determines our sex, culture determines our gender.

Gender refers not to our anatomy, but our behaviour as socially programmed men and women. She adds that feminist activity is aimed at promoting the position of women's equality and gender issues play a part in every aspect of human production.

In this chapter, the author will employ radical feminism theory to interrogate whether women are economically, socially and psychologically oppressed in novels, plays, poetry and African folk lore or oral literature.

3:2 Feminism and the Novel

Literary writers the world over have used the novel as a vehicle to critique male dominance and relegation of women. Since the novel is studied in many countries to bolster language competence among students, novelists use it as a vehicle to discourage domestic violence, dowry, male chauvinism, female circumcision and other practices that run counter to the position of women in the society. Both male and female novelists write to convey feminist tenets using the novel. Ole Kulet in *Blossoms of the Savannah* attacks patriarchy, which manifests through female circumcision and bureaucracy in the family. He satirizes male characters using caricatures like Oloisudori, Olarinkoi and Ole Kaelo by portraying them as greedy and unscrupulous ingrates with obsession for materialism and sex without regard for the woman's life. Oloisudori has six wives and wants Resian, ole Kaelo's daughter for the seventh wife. Olarinkoi who initially poses as Resian's saviour from the father's oppression turns on her and attempts to rape her. Generally, male characters in *Blossoms of the Savannah* are portrayed as robbers, rapists, brutes, fools, oppressors while women as visionary, loving, intelligent, oppressed and understanding. Apparently, this is a feminist attempt to elevate the position of women. The dominant themes in feminist novels are patriarchy, gender inequalities, domestic violence, obsolete traditions, male chauvinism, gender parity, role of women and other themes relevant to women issues. Apart from Ole Kulet, other feminist novelists include Marjorie O Macgoye, Margaret Ogola, Nawal El Saadawi, Tsitsi Dangarebgwa, Toni Morrison, Nuruddin Farah, Buchi Emecheta, just to mention a few. Our analysis of feminist novels begins from a global level and then turn to regional levels.

3:2.1 Gender Differences in Slave Characters: a Feminist Critique of Toni Morrison's *Beloved* and *Narrative of the Life of Frederic Douglass, an American Slave*

Feminist scholars have grappled with the question of gender differences among slaves in the Americas in the seventeenth and eighteenth centuries. Whereas some scholars hold that both male and female salves were assigned different roles, feminist scholars such as Angela Davis hold that "[e]nslaved women labored no less than enslaved men" (105). She observes that unlike white women, female slaves performed the same roles as men slaves. Adrienne Davis reiterates this argument that "[i]n the middle of the nineteenth century seven-eighths of enslaved people regardless of sex were field workers. In 1800 when Santee Canal was built in North Carolina, enslaved women constituted 50% of the construction crew" (106).

Published in 1845, *Narrative of the life of Frederick Douglass, an American Slave* is the gruesome tale of the life of Frederic Douglass, a slave who suffers the harrowing experiences of slavery in the American city of Maryland. He reveals horrible acts committed by slave masters on male and female slaves, for example murder, torture and exploitation. After hiring his labour out and being forced to give his wages to the master, he rebels and then flees to the free north in the United States of America. Born in Tukahoe of a white slave master and black slave woman, in the south of the United States, Douglass is denied the right to the knowledge of his parentage, deprived of the mother's first love among other cruel elements of slavery. In spite of their Christian faith, the slave masters display the callousness inconsistent to the Christian teaching of love and compassion. They assault the slaves on daily basis and shoot some of them. Fed up by the cruelty of the masters, Douglass flees the south to the free north and joins the anti slavery campaign. In this subsection, we will use Frederic Douglass' characters to distinguish the roles of women slaves from those of men.

Toni Morrison's *Beloved* is the story of a female slave, Sethe who lives in Cincinnati in the United States. Sethe, a former slave, had four children with Halle, a fellow slave and Babby Sugg's son. Baby Sugg's labored as a slave for many years until her son, Halle worked hard and bought her freedom. After the death of their master, Mr. Garner, who practiced a benevolent form of slavery, his brother, a school teacher, takes charge of the farm and reintroduces a dehumanizing slavery, for instance raping and milking female slaves in the presence of their male partners. Halle runs mad after witnessing the violation of his wife, Sethe and the murder of Sixo, a fellow slave. Expecting her fourth child, Denver, Sethe sets off to her mother-in-law's home in the north. Along the way, she collapses out of exhaustion but is assisted by Army Denver, a white girl. She helps her deliver her baby in a boat and Sethe names the baby, Denver. She receives further help from Stamp Paid who rows her across Ohio River to Baby Sugg's house. On the 28 days of her stay, school teacher arrives prepared to take Sethe back to the slave farm. Determined to save her children from the yoke of slavery, Sethe resolves to kill them. The baby dies and Sethe is jailed but the abolitionists fight for her release. The ghost of the baby she killed, who she now name, Beloved, comes back to haunt her. This study examines Morrison's characters such as Sethe, Paul D, Halle and Babby Suggs to analyse gender differences between male and female slaves in the novel.

3:2.2 Gender Differences in the *Narrative of Life Frederic Douglass, an American Slave.*

Scholars of American slavery observe that female slaves were assigned different roles in the United States of America. Allen William in a US' congress task force report entitled "History of Slave Laborers in the Construction of the United States Capitol" notes that men slaves were used to construct the White house and got involved in activities like "coaxing stone from the earth without power tools of any kind; transporting, hauling, and carving... the enslaved work men had to endure isolation, loneliness in addition to their rigorous labors," (6). It is evident that the slave system reserved certain tasks for men because the tasks demanded more energy that female slaves did not possess. William adds that the commissioner in charge of construction of the Whitehouse advertised on the newspaper:

> Wanted to Hire, for next year to work on the Free stone
> Quarries lately occupied by Public on Acquia Creek,
> Sixty strong active Negro men (6).

Female slaves are not wanted in this instance because the working conditions are not favourable for them. William asserts that the quarries were located in a snake infested island and nearby areas that swarmed with mosquitoes. He adds that the men slaves specialized in "mortar making, plastering, and carpentry". On the plantations, they went around "building, repairing tobacco barns, cowsheds, hog houses, chicken coops, corn cribs, granaries, dairies and smoke houses" (12). On the other hand, Edmund Morgan cites two roles for women slaves that were imported to offset the sexual imbalance on white farms: "to make children and tobacco" (26). The making of children crowned her the most essential asset to her slave master. Angela Davis clarifies the female slave's role saying:

> The African slave woman was charged with keeping the home in order… as her biological destiny, the woman bore the fruits of procreation. As her social destiny, she cooked, sewed, washed, cleaned house and raised children". (5)

It is clear that the female slave was relegated to more domestic roles, for instance household chores such as cooking, washing and raising children. She also bore slave children to be sold or hired out by the master. Davis notes that the slave and his labour did not belong to himself or her self. He or she did everything for the benefit of the master.

Slave masters therefore assigned male and female slaves different roles. In his autobiography, *Narrative of the Life of Frederick Douglass, an American Slave* the author presents to us instances where gender differences among slaves were apparent. Slave masters assigned female slaves childcare roles where they ordered them to attend to babies with ultimate care. In the narrative, there is the instance of Fred's wife's cousin. Mr. Gile's wife, Hick, instructs her to mind her baby. Overwhelmed by a three-day's fatigue, she sleeps and lets the baby to cry. What follows is shocking. Mrs. Hick seizes an oak stick of wood by the fireplace and hits the girl on the nose and breast. She breaks her nose and breast, leading to a tragic end of her life (15). On the other hand, the male slaves in the story are assigned different roles. They are assigned field activities like looking after livestock, ploughing the farm with oxen, clearing bushes and others. The slave master, Mr. Covey, for instance, sends Frederick to the woods with oxen but the oxen smash the cart. When he returns, Covey rushes at him with the fierceness of a tiger, tears off his clothes and lashes at him… "cutting him savagely" (36). Male slaves are also free to learn skills like carpentry and masonry to hire them out. Frederick Douglass is an electrician and hires his skills over the weekend. However as a slave he is forced to bring all the proceeds to his slave master. The difference extends to breeding of slaves. In Frederick Douglass' story, the masters tag female slaves as breeders and sell them out. But the male slaves are just hired for a period of time. Master Covey bought Caroline, a female slave, as a breeder. He hires a male partner at a price to breed slave children to multiply his wealth (37). Whereas the male slave returns after one year, the female slave, Caroline will remain in the home to proliferate Mr. Covey's property by giving birth to slaves. Adrienne Davis observes that American slavery used the black woman slave to "reproduce the slave workforce through giving birth and serving as forced sexual labor to countless men of all races" (105). They were forced to have sex with both white and black men to replicate the slave population for profit.

Willie Lee Rose in her book *Slavery and Freedom* observes that there were many gender specific differences in slavery. The female slaves during the middle passage did not travel in holds below the deck but sea men allowed them to walk about the quarterdeck without shackles to be easily accessible to their sexual desires. (16). Once they were put up for sale, the most highly prized women were fertile women of childbearing age. In his letter to Joel Yancy, Thomas Jefferson, a former US president, frankly stated that he "considered a woman who brings a child every two years as more profitable than the best man on the farm for what she produces is an addition to the capital while the man's labour disappears in mere consumption." (42-43). However, the men slaves were always more expensive than women slaves. Therefore, the ratio of men slaves to women slaves soared to 2:1.

Deborah White expounds that once purchased, the slave masters put "women to labor or used them as concubines or wives to male slaves" (37). The women also worked in the fields, nursed children, were midwives, seamstresses, house cooks, children's cooks- working ten hours a day. Pregnant slaves were treated better, not because the master cared, but because she brought into the world an important addition to the capital. Once a woman was past child caring age, she would work like everyone else until the age of sixty-five when she would be freed. Rose observes that Men slaves went through different experiences even during the middle passage. Scared of their physical strength, the slave masters bound them in steel and kept them below the decks. The slave masters did not prize men for their fertility but for their health and ability to perform hard labour. They were taught tasks to be drivers, blacksmiths, stablemen, carpenters, ditch men, skilled craftsmen and others. Engineers gave them a chance to move more often than women slaves did. The skills enabled them to hire themselves out, earn money, half of which went to master, although they finally bought their freedom.

3.2.3 Gender Differences in Morrison's *Beloved*

In Tony Morrison's *Beloved*, she clearly depicts gender differences between men and women slaves. Although sometimes the roles overlap, they differ to some extent. As earlier mentioned Morrison's, *Beloved* is a heart-renting story of Sethe, a woman slave who escapes the brutality of slave masters at Kentucky to freedom at Cincinnati. Through the eyes of the heroine, her mother and mother-in-law, Babby Suggs, the roles of female slaves are clearly distinguished from those of male slaves such as her husband, Halle, and his colleagues like Paul D, Sixo and others. The dehumanizing roles that slaves play cause a deep sense of alienation- estrangement from the self or rather internal fragmentation. Ali, H. (2013) observes that *Beloved's* "fragmented structure" gives a hint of the characters' sense of alienation that is a consequence of the dehumanizing nature of slavery (p.1422). Morrison uses a number of flashbacks that disrupt the chronological order of events.

Sethe's earlier experiences on Mr Garner's farm depict gender differences between male and female slaves. The slave master sees Sethe as a breeder at Sweet Home. Schoolteacher values her for her fertility and that is why he tracks her down all the way to Cincinnati. Her children are being 'raised as property to do the work that Sweet Home desperately needed". Schoolteacher says he is glad she has ten breeding years (p.184). As Thomas Jefferson asserted, female slaves were breeders bought to reproduce more slaves. Baby Suggs, Sethe's mother-in-law had eight children with six fathers (p.29). The narrator says:

> Her two girls, neither of whom had
> Their adult teeth were sold and gone
> And she had not been able to wave good bye.

These gender roles, as aforementioned depict the dehumanizing nature of slavery or slavery's destruction of people's identity. African people were reduced into mere property to be replicated like money and fixed assets. Baby Suggs is just like a cow that births eight calves from six bulls to be owned by the farmer. Men slaves on the other hand were also used to reproduce children on the farm by inbreeding. Poor slave masters who could afford to hire men slaves for breeding or too unfeeling to care, forced sons to have sex with their mothers to birth more slaves. In the story, Baby Suggs is happy with Mr. Garner's type of slavery because he does not bring her sons to the cabin to have sex with her as they did in Carolina' (p.173). On the other hand, masters did not sell men out as breeders but their sex was just rented out to reproduce strong slaves for their masters. Not all men slaves married. Baby Suggs wonders whether Mr. Garner would pick wives or her sons or will leave their libido to run wild. In fact, they have sex with cows. The dehumanizing nature of slavery is depicted again. The inbreeding, done at Carolina reduces Africans to animals. Do we not see Billy goats climbing their mothers? To white people at this time, blacks were just like animals. There is also the theme of racial prejudice. Furthermore, female slaves did household chores. They assisted their mistresses in everything. Baby Suggs assisted Mrs. Garner to do all household chores. The two of them cooked, washed, ironed, made candles, clothes, soap and cider, fed chickens, pigs, dogs, geese, milked cows, churned butter, rendered fat and fires. (p.172)

In other cases, women attended to multiple roles. They did all household chores and worked the field like men slaves. Morrissey Marietta observes that shortage of labour, particularly towards the end of slave trade prompted slave owners to use "women slaves as field labourers rather than household workers" (3). The women were all the time confined on the farm. They could not hire themselves out to make money for fear that men would have sex with them. The female slave Aunt Herster in the *Narrative of Life of Frederick Douglass* is a one such example. She goes out with a male friend and when she returns, the master "stripped her to the waist and commenced to lay on the heavy cow skin and soon the warm, red blood came dripping to the floor," (p.6). In Tony Morrison's novel, Sethe's mother always worked the field. Sethe saw her very few times. By the time she woke up, her mother was in line. If the moon was bright, they worked by its light. On Sunday, "she could sleep like a stick." (p.75). But this could not satisfy the master's demands, she had to satisfy the sexual desires of white men. The aim of the sexual exploitation of the female slave was to the attack on the slave community. It was a means through which the slave masters expressed their weird sovereignty on the black community and emasculate the black man. Angel Davis observes that the sexual exploitation was part of "slavery's utilization of productive capacities of every man, woman, child... and through it, the black woman was wholly integrated into the productive force" (p. 6). She had to participate in the provision of labour for material production and also birth children to increase the labour force for the master.

On the way to Americas, the seamen had sex with the female slave (Sethe's mother) and she gave birth to colored children. The old woman Nan says that they were together with Sethe's mother at sea: "Both were take up many times by the crew" (p. 78). But when she bore children, she loved Sethe most.

> She threw them away but you
> The one from the crew she threw away
> One on the island
> Without names, she threw them
> You she gave the name of the black man
> She put her arms around him.

In addition to this, female slaves could hang babies using baskets on trees to work on the fields at Sweet Home (p. 196). Moses Grandy in his slave narrative entitled *Narrative of life of Moses Grandy*, observes "[w]omen who had sucking children suffered much from their breasts becoming full of milk, the infants being left... 'I have seen the overseer beat them with raw hide so that the blood and milk flew mingled from their breasts" (p. 18). Being a woman was therefore a double burden in slavery. Nonetheless, men acquired skills they could hire out on other farms to make money for the slave master and slaves. Halle, Sethe's husband sympathizes with her mother, whose hip is hurt. He hires his skills on other farms every Sunday for five years to buy his mother's freedom. The gender differences in this context depict the theme of exploitation. The master exploited the female slave both sexually and physically. She met the master's sex desires and worked in the field. Sethe's mother is compelled to hang her baby on a tree to work on the field too. The men slaves with skills work and give their money to the master.

There are also gender differences between men and women slaves in transit from one place to another. As earlier mentioned by scholar Rose Willie, during their journey from Africa to Americas, women slaves were given freedom to walk in the ship to be accessible to seamen's sexual desires. Nan says she and Sethe's mother 'were take up many times by the crew." Apparently, they did not travel below the deck like men slaves but walked without shackles. The slave masters chained and placed men slaves below the deck. They move male slave Paul D in the novel from Kentucky to Georgia on a torturous journey. It is after he tried to kill his new master, Mr. Brandywine. They chain forty-six prisoners and flank them, armed with rifles. They shoot men slaves when they ask for breakfast.

"Want some breakfast, nigger?"
"Yes, sir."
"Hungry nigger?"
"Yes sir".
"Here you go."

He is shot (p. 132). The theme of oppression is evident in the two instances. The man carries the seed and therefore the symbol of a particular community. Men slaves are symbols of the black race and since the whites want them exterminated, they oppress them and have sex with their women.

Finally, women slaves were subjected to sexual abuses and many others to humiliate them and men slaves. The worst humiliation over a tribe or nation is to abuse their wives and daughters sexually as they watch. Dubois attacks the sexual barbarity of the white race:

> I shall forgive the south much in its final judgment day:
> I shall forgive its slavery- for slavery is a world old habit
> I shall forgive its fighting for a well lost cause and remembering that
> Struggle with tender tears, I shall forgive its so called "pride of race", the
> passion of its hot blood- but one thing I shall never forgive, neither in this
> world nor the world to come is its wanton and persistent insulting of black woman hood. (p.172)

The female slave Baby Suggs is compelled to have sex with her master to keep her third born with her. She conceived the master's child and the boy, traded for lumber. Mr Garner is only interested in meeting his sex urge, but not in assisting the slave woman. (29). Schoolteacher takes Sethe to a stable and milks her. He gives the milk to white babies. She says, "They held me down and took it, milk that belonged to my baby (172). The milking is done in the presence of Halle, the husband. The white men demascularize men slaves, they take away their traditional role of dominating and protecting their wives. In spite of Halle loving his wife, Sethe says:

> They took my milk
> And he saw it

> And didn't come
> If he is alive
> And he saw that, he would not
> Step foot at my door,
> Not Halle. (85)

The last words on this utterance suggest sexual abuse thereby hurting Halle irrevocably. He ran mad after this experience. It does not end with Sethe. The female slave Ella is locked up in a room and two white men use her- father and son. For a full year, the two abused her in turns (146). The writer suggests that slavery destroys the identity of both the oppressed and the oppressor. Halle runs mad but the white man also loses his status as a person. Ella's incident is bizarre. A father and a son share the same woman like goats. As the slavemasters abuse their powers, they lose their identity. A beast kills a hungry other like in Paul D's experience.

3.5 Conclusion

In peculiar instances the roles of male and female slaves overlapped, for example they all worked in the fields. Nevertheless, male and female slaves played different roles by reason of the patriarchal nature of the slave system. The exploitation leveled against the woman slave was both sexual for pleasure and profit as opposed to the man who only offered labour on the farm. The violation and milking of Sethe in the stable and her mother's sexual abuse en route to Americas are classical examples.

3:6 Feminist Critique of Oral Literature

Although feminism is used in critiquing modern literature, we can also use it to examine African folklore to deconstruct patriarchal attitudes underlying the tales. The theory perambulates all genres of orature.

3:6.1 Feminism and Oral narratives

Read the following story and write a Feminist Critique:

> There lived a beautiful girl called Sela. The story of her beauty visited every home in the world. But Sela loved pleasure. She loved song and dance; she adored *ilitungu*. *She* would surrender her soul to any man who knew how to play it. One day, Mwambu, her elder brother, went for a stroll. When he reached the river, he saw Sela picking *enderema*; he got elated. He knew that in the evening he would have a meal he had missed for a very long time. At supper time, Mwambu bounced in, braced to enjoy enderema only to find the usual cowpeas.
>
> "Where is the *enderema* I saw you picking?" thundered Mwambu.
> "I didn't go to the river today," replied Sela.
> "You're a liar!" roared Mwambu and slapped her.
> Sela wept and returned to the kitchen. She did not blame her brother; he rarely beat her. She resolved to visit the river to unearth the root of her troubles. She rose at sun rise and headed for the river. She found a dark fat girl, exactly like her picking *enderema*. Sela was very veeery shocked. She had met her own ghost. Reliving her fate the previous night, she decided to greet the girl.
> "*Mulembe yaya.*"
> "*Mulembe swa.*"
> "Me, they call me Sela," she introduced herself.
> "I am also Sela," the stranger, said.

They embraced, both surprised.

Sela told the stranger the experience she had had the previous evening. Sela 2 agreed that he had seen a man pass by with a gaze that suggested that he knew her. She proceeded to welcome her to their home but warned her that she was the only human being in a family of monsters. When they reached home, Sela Two said that the man eaters had gone hunting and would return with song and dance."

"When they come," instructed Sela Two, "don't come out however sweet their songs are."

"I won't," affirmed Sela One.

"I'll dig a pit in the compound and hide you there," suggested Sela Two, "and don't be tempted by the moving songs please."

"I won't sister," persisted Sela One.

After the evening meal, Sela Two dug a deep pit behind the store and hid Sela One there. She covered the mouth with banana leaves. The ogres arrived, lively. The home was thrown astir with merry songs and dances accompanied by crotchet beats of the drums. They thumped their feet, shook their shoulders and clapped their hands; the result was a moving *kamabeka* dance. Their voices mixed well to produce a harmonious song. They sniffed their noses around and caught a visitor's scent in the home. They sang a song to express it:

Sela mekeni muya kaunya muno
Sela mukeni muya kaunya muno
Sela mukeni muya kaunya muno
Sela mukeni muya kaunya muno

Sela we've smelt a visitor's scent
Sela we've smelt a visitor's scent

Sela we've smelt a visitor's scent
Sela we've smelt a visitor's scent

Sela Two was astonished at their sensitivity and sang another moving song to dissuade them that there was no visitor on the compound. She named them one by one:

Okanakhundia papa okanakhundia
Okanakhundia Wamukobe okanakhundia
Okanakhundia Wamalabe okanakhundia
Okanakhundia mukeni kamayena

Want to swallow me dad want to swallow me
Want to swallow me Wamukobe want to swallow me
Want to swallow me Wamukobe want to swallow me
Want to swallow brothers, where do I find a visitor?

Sela's voice was sweet but it did not convince the monsters. They enlivened their dance and thumped their feet with an amazing passion. What vigour! They plucked their *matungus* skillfully; Sela One inside the pit died of pleasure. She swayed her body to the slightest change of rhythm. She forgot all her fears. She forgot warnings. Those sweet voices that soothed her passion would not kill her. It was Sela Two's sheer jealousy to deny her a moment of happiness. She danced, danced and danced. She climbed up the pit, threw away the banana leaves and joined the frisky dance. The ogres rejoiced to see the food and danced more vigorously:

Sela we've smelt the visitor's scent
Sela we've smelt the visitor's scent
What we said was true

Sela we smelt the visitor's scent.

The ogres then began licking Sela; the foolish girl thought they were attracted to her. They stopped licking her and tore her skin. They stopped singing and scrambled over the parts of her body. She whimpered and called Sela Two to no avail. Nobody could save her from the hands of these man eaters. They ate all her flesh, deserted the bones in front of the store and went to sleep.

The following morning, Sela Two woke up and seeing her friend's bones wept at her foolishness. How could she risk her life for a dance? She went to the bush and plucked a branch from the tree, *lufufu*. She arranged the bones in position and lashed them. Sela One came back to life. Sela Two warned her never to be lured by song. She vowed to obey.

Whenever the monsters came and sung their song, Sela would sing her song and they would apologize:

Ndomakhandio luweni ndomakhandio
Ndomakhandio Kichwa ndomakhandio
I'm just joking Luweni I,m just joking.
I,m just joking Kichwa I,m just joking

Sela One would not come out of the pit. Days went on. One day SelaOne said,

"Come with me so that you live with human beings. It's hard to stay with ogres."

Sela Two agreed on condition that nobody called her ogre.

They reached home and Mwambu was very elated to welcome them. He found it very hard to distinguish between them but her sister had a gap in the teeth that Sela Two lacked. After few days, he married Sela Two vowing never to call her ogre. But one day after drinking *busaa,* Mwambu stood up and shouted, "these are the disadvantages of being born among ogres!"

Sela Two picked a rope, ran to the banana farm and hanged herself. (Nyongesa, 2018, p. 35-39)

The above oral narrative has certain attributes that demean the position of the woman in the society. First, cooking and the kitchen is the role of the woman. Mwambu is a young man who cannot go to the kitchen and cook the vegetable he wants. He has to cast tirades at his siter and even slap her over the vegetable he would have gathered at the river, cooked and served by himself. The boy child in the society from which the story is derived is being socialed to be a master and the girl as a slave. The parents do not even reprimand Mwambu for this. There is also a signal of domestic violence or wife battering; Mwambu is being socialized to become a wife batterer. He does not control his tempers because when Sela One tells her that she did not go to the river, Mwambu lets his temper to flare like a beast.

Secondly, we learn that the ogres in the story are men. Since the ogres have mystic powers, men are being associated with mystery while the woman, Sela Two, who is their sister, does not have any such powers. While the men go out to hunt and explore the world, Sela Two has to remain at home. This is an indictment at the woman- she is weak and therefore the home is her sphere of influence. Only men are allowed to be outgoing, but the girl has to remain at home and will go out to fetch firewood or water for the men to use when they return. Sela Two can only go out to gather *enderema* at the river.

Thirdly, Sela One's visit at Sela two's home reveals other prejudices against women. When the ogres sing and dance, Sela Two cannot school her emotions. She likes the songs so much that she ignores Sela One's warning and comes out of the hideout. The community believes that women are so emotional and gullible that they can be cheated by petty gifts to lose their lives. The men are potrayed as clever and can cheat women by a few words and then abuse them sexually. The licking and consequent murder signifies sexual abuse- particularly rape. Feminists will interpret Sela Two's intervention that women can only be saved by fellow women. Men cannot be trusted including Mwambu, Sela One's sister. He vows to keep the secret never to tell anyone that Sela Two's siblings are ogres. But when he is drunk, he shouts at the rooftop.

3:6.2 Feminism and Riddles

The following riddles have something to do with the position of women in Swahili communities where they are derived:

> Challenge: I have a wife; everybody she bears has a beard.
> Response: The maize plant.
> Challenge: My mother has given birth in the bush.
> Response: Pineapple
> Challenge: My daughter who gives birth by excreting on the ground.
> Response: The Pumpkin (Miruka, 1994, 31).

In the above riddles, the woman's major role is reproduction, which runs counter to tenets of feminism. It underscores the position of the woman as a leader, professional and other positions that men hold in the society. Feminist scholars see such riddles as an attempt to socialize female children as sex objects that will only exult in child bearing and achieve nothing more to help them pursue self-actualization. Whereas these communities prize fertility as the crown of women, feminist criticism demands that men should also be valued by their fertility to enhance gender equity. Let us examine the riddles below:

Challenge: A small married woman who cooks better than your mother.
Response: The honey bee.
Challenge: I have a very good girl but she is untouchable.
Response: Fire.
Challenge: The dirty Fatuma.
Response: The broom.
Challenge: Mother carry me.
Response: The bed
Challenge: My daughter who leaves hungry but returns full.
Response: The water pot
Challenge: My daughter who has one eye on the head.
Response: The needle. (Miruka, 1994, P. 31-32)

Feminist tenets decry the background beliefs in the creation of these riddles. In these communities the woman's role is homemaking and the children are socialized to believe so. The first riddle implies that the woman is a cook and she is compared to a bee that tirelessly prepares honey in the beehive. Why are men not mentioned in relation to cooking? Are they unable to cook? It is a social construction to limit women to the kitchen and reserve better roles for men. The second riddle identifies cooking fire with women and girls. It tells the girl child to grow up knowing that she will always be closer to the cooking place in her life, which feminists dispute.

The third riddle suggests that all chores related to cleaning are reserved for women and girls: scrubbing the floor, sweeping the house, washing clothes (husband's and children's and hers), bathing the children and keeping herself clean. Men are not supposed to do anything related to cleaning in the home hence associating the broom with the woman (Fatuma). Osman or Baraka cannot be dirty; however, shabby they look because they are men.

The fourth riddle reserves all child caring roles like babysitting, baby feeding, baby soothing for women. Men will take professional jobs and businesses as women stick around babies all day long. The image of the bed signifies the bedroom woman's sphere of influence. On the bed, she will conceive her children; on the bed she will lay them; on the bed she will sort out dirty clothes and bedding. It is a fulcrum of her world and many will reprimand a woman who cannot make a bed; no man will be condemned for such reason.

The fifth and sixth riddle reserves all house chores for women and girls. The water pot and needle represent chores like fetching water, washing clothes, repairing torn clothes, ironing, cleaning utensils and many others. The inner rooms of the house and the kitchen are the woman's sphere of influence, which is gender bias. For feminists, these chores should be attended by men too.

3:6.3 Feminism and Oral Poetry

In oral poetry, feminist tenets are expressed. Let us analyse the following song:

> We women will never have peace,
> We will never prosper; the troubles from men are ceaseless,
> At night they are worse.
> He stands his bicycle,
> He calls me, I respond,
> My man hurls insults at my mother;
> The troubles from men are ceaseless,
> At night they are worse.
> He drinks to his full,

And vomits on me;
When shall we have peace?
The troubles from men are ceaseless,
My house is spotlesslessly clean,
My man does not see it,
The troubles from men are ceaseless,
At night they are worse;
He carries a bull gonorrhoea from the town
And smears it in my body,
We shall never have peace,
The pain is terrible,
At night it is worse.
I even bore him children,
My man bothers my head
With stupid words,
At night he is worse;
We women will never have peace,
We will never prosper, the troubles from men are ceaseless,
At night they are worse. (Miruka, 1994, P. 99)

The singer in this song tells the audience that women are oppressed; they are the *other* in the marriage setting. The persona, a married woman, complains that women face many problems right from sex in marriage. The men control sex and they will have it when they want, not when the woman wants it. As soon the man experiences an erection, the woman must submit. The singer uses the metaphor "he stands his bicycle" to signify a penile erection and calls her to submit. In the feminist perspective, this is rape because the woman should have sex when she is willing and ready. The men in this society therefore rape their wives because they demand for sex without caring whether the wives are ready for it or not.

The men do not assist in household chores, the women clean the houses. However, when the men arrive from town, they dirty the houses with boots. They are deliberately careless and reckless to prove the point that they are masters over the women. Whereas they insist on faithfulness in women, the men are unfaithful. They visit brothels in towns and get infected with sexually transmitted diseases, which they pass on to their wives. Moreover, the men are arrogant; in spite of the wives bearing them children, they insult the wives and worse still, their wives' mothers. In is absurd to note that these men do not insult their wives' fathers. The entire spite is directed at women. The persona concludes that women will never have peace and prosperity if patriarchal dominance is not curtailed.

3:7 Feminist Critique of Poetry

Modern poets have written poems to either portray the oppression of the woman or elevate the role of women in the society. In this section we will use two examples to show the influence of feminism in poetry.

Mother of Children
A.D Amateshe

She rummages through her life
For what the children will eat;
From the break of dawn to dusk
She juggles the little at hand
To feed the spilling household.

Her hands, blistered with labour
Till the unyielding piece of land;
From the start of rains to drought

> She gleans the grains of hardship
> To fill the barrel of tolerance.
>
> Her feet, roughened by treks,
> Walk the unending paths of struggle;
> From the turn of day to the turn of night
> The endless search for water
> Takes her beyond the emaciated hills
>
> Through the wilderness of the plain
> Her mind wonders about the man
> Long gone with the hunting season;
> Her melodious voice fills the air
> Bringing hope to the sullen children.
>
> Daughter of the Toling clan,
> Donor of cattle to your father's homestead,
> The cocks are crwing for you
> To get up from your rugged bed
> For another hardening day ... (Amateshe, 1989, p.125)

In this poem, Amateshe underscores the pivotal role of the woman in the society. Her ability to provide especially after the loss of the father is particularly stunning. However, when the poem is placed under feminist scrutiny, we realize that there is shocking oppression of the woman in the society. The woman has to labour endlessly to feed the "spilling household", which suggests that the late husband sired many children and might have possibly passed on owing to failure to cope with the pressures to raise the children. The man is portrayed as irresponsible and weak because he cannot plan his family and is unable to bear with the pressure that comes with the demands to raise the family.

In the second stanza, the woman has multiple roles in attempt to uplift the economy of the home. She plants, weeds and harvests crops; as a result, her "hands are blistered" with labour. From the farm, she has to travel long distances to fetch water to prepare food and clean clothes and the house. Above all, she has to sing songs of hope to keep off depressive memories from the orphans under her care. In the last stanza, there is a reference to brideprice. The persona describes her as the "donor of cattle" to her father's homestead, which to feminists is commodification of women. She has been sold in the matrimonial home to slave for the weak man who dies early to leave her in despair. She has to wake up at cockcrow from "the rugged bed" to slave for another day. In feminist perspective, Amateshe's poem depicts oppression of women and by the end of their lives even the children they have toiled to raise may never assist them.

Chuma Mmeka

> He shows a might out of wrong
> Wanting it his way, not as it is right to be
> He basks in the ruins of an obnoxious time
> Yearning to lord over, he puts her far under
> His will is command, hers is just to obey
> Her saunters off to school and then to work
> She lives in the kitchen and the other room
> He returns to play and to the news
> She serves the food and to the sex
> He takes delight in fertilizing conception
> And she left with the pains of the labour
> He mutilates her to keep her chaste

While he goes to sow his wild oats
Enslave her, check her; oh that's not abusive!
She is weaker and he is strong and protective
Hear now, all ye he! Wallow not in foolery!
Be not deceived by the gentlest of her looks
For she indeed stays the strongest in spirit
She is dynamically and stupifyingly gifted
Her wisest can take his nastiest stupidity
Yet her smallest can drop him in the purse
She has reached a climax above his zenith
And had had many him bowing to her
Give honor, without her he would not be
Watch it! She may yet still be his future (Mwanaka & Purificação, 2018, P. 32)

Mmeka's poem begins by a shocking depiction of oppression of the wife by the husband. The persona says the man dictates everything in the marriage and does not admit even where he is wrong. He holds on outdated traditions that encourage him to be totalitarian (He basks in the ruins of an obnoxious time). Such traditions hold that it is the man's to command and the woman's to obey. The man does white collar jobs like teaching at school as the wife sticks to the kitchen to cook and serve food and give him sex in the bedroom. The men encourage female genital mutilation to lower the libido of the women, but they loiter around to sleep with other women (while he goes to sow his wild oats). The man is suspicious and spies on the wife, checks her messages on the phone and tracks her communication and movement. When questioned, he claim, "oh that's not abusive/She is weaker and he is strong and protective."

The persona now starts enumerating the strengths of the woman. Although she looks weak, men should not be deceived, she is stronger, in fact, she is wise enough to tolerate his stupidity and will easily drop men into her purse. She can lead them by the nose to empty their bank accounts into hers. Many men kneel before the woman and she ought to be revered because without her, men cannot exist. They are born of women and she is the future of our society.

REFERENCES

Amateshe A. (1989). *Introduction to East African Poetry.* Nairobi. EAEP

Ali, H. (2013). Gender Analysis in Toni Morrison's *Beloved* and *Sila.Middle Journal of Scientific Researc,. 16.10*: P. 1419-1423.

Bois, D. (1920). *Darkwater: Voices from Within the Veil.* New York. Harcourt, Brace.

Davis, A. (2002). The sexual Economy of American Slavery.MA Thesis University of Toronto.

Davis, A. (1971).The Black Woman's Role in the Community of Slaves.*Journal of Black Studies and Research,3.4*: 1-10.

Davis, A. (1983). *Women, Race,and Class.* New York. Random House.

Douglass, F. (1990).*Narrative of the Life of Frederick Douglass.*New York. Dover publications.

Grandy, M. (1843).*Narrative of the Life of Moses Grandy: Late a Slave in the United States of America.* London: Gilpin.

Jafferson, T. (1953).Letter from Thomas Jefferson to Joel Yancy. In *Thomas Jefferson's Farm Book: with Commentary and Relevant Extracts from other Writings.* Ed. Edwin Morris Betts. Princeton UP.

Marrietta, M. (1984).Women's work, family and Reproduction among Caribbean Slaves.

Working Paper 76. Texas Tech University, P. 1-10.

Miruka O. (1994). *Encounter with Oral Literature.*Nairobi. EAEP.

Morgan, E (1972). Slavery and Freedom: The American Paradox. *Journal of American History,*

59 :1-27.
Morrison, T. (1991). *Beloved.* New York. Penguin Group.
Mwanaka, T & Purificação, D (2018). *Best "New" African Poets 2017 Anthology.* Chitungwiza: Mwanaka Media and Publishing.
Nyongesa A. (2018). *The Water Cycle.* Chitungwiza: Mwanaka Media and Publishing.
Rose, W. (1982).*Slavery and Freedom.* New York. Cambridge UP.
Tyson, L (2006). *Critical Theory.*New York. Routledge.
White, D. (1985).*Aren't I a woman? Female Slaves in the Plantation South.* New York. Nortan and Co, New York.

CHAPTER FOUR:

Postcolonial Criticism

4.1 Introduction

"Colonialism is a systematised negation of the other, a frenzied attempt to deny the other any attribute of humanity...which if left unchallenged[...] the colonized's defenses collapse and many of them end up in psychiatric institutions," (182) observes Fanon (1961) in attempt to emphasize the need for resistance against foreign, dominant cultures. In his works, Fanon proposed resistance against colonial influence from within and without.

During and after colonialism, African, literary writers used literature to resist the dominant, orientalist, degrading discourses of the time. Inspired by postcolonial writers such as Frantz Fanon, they viewed literature as a way of routing out demeaning notions that had been inculcated among the colonized by the colonizers. African literary writers chose two strategies of resistance: cultural fixity and cultural hybridity. Those who chose cultural fixity underscored the need to glorify Africa's past traditions to combat colonialism, which had alienated and dehumanized Africans. Leopold Senghor and Aime Ceisar came up with the Negritude movement that glorified African culture to restore the self esteem of Africans, which they had lost during colonialism. Poets like Kofi Awoonor and Okot P' Bitek joined this movement. However, literary writers such as Christopher Okigbo and Wole Shoyinka rejected Negritude movement because they saw themselves as poets of two worlds: The West and Africa. This brand of poets therefore opted for cultural hybridity, a form of resistance that embraced the two cultures. The paper explores strategies of resistence in the poetry of Okot P' Bitek and Christopher Okigbo; using the postcolonial theory, it analyses elements of hybridity and fixity in the works of the two poets

Most African literary writers at independence wrote to depict the beauty and perfection of African culture as resistance to derogatory and oppressive colonial writing. Ngugi Wa Thiong'o, for example, had set himself against orientalist philosophy of colonialism that he opposed the use of foreign languages in African Literature. With Obi Wali and Chinweizu, they proposed that African writers should write literature in African languages to ensure that literature is connected to a people's revolutionary struggle against colonialism. For them, the use of African languages would make African writers dangerous to colonial powers because they are directly speaking to the people but writing in European languages would be crippling. Thiong'o (1986) holds that language was at the centre of imperialism. He notes that whereas "the bullet was the means of physical subjugation, language was the means of spiritual subjugation" (9). Fanon (1961), *Wretched of the Earth,* asserts that the African writer addresses his own people, clarifies themes and dwells on those that are "typically nationalist [....] a literature of combat to mould national consciousness" (159). On the contrary, there were African literary writers who opted for the middle ground to blend African and European style in writing literature. This study explores resistance strategies in the poetry of Okot P' Bitek and Christopher Okigbo; using the postcolonial theory, it analyses hybridity and fixity as modes of resistance.

4.2 Definition of post colonialism

Ashcroft (1995) and his colleagues observe, "[i]t is a theory that studies the cultural, intellectual realities and tensions that occurred in many nations from the beginning of colonial contact" (p. 1). It emerged when the colonized started to reflect and express tension which followed after disruption by the mixture of imperial culture and native ways. Post-colonialism and its prominent theorists have contributed to migration literature by identifying a framework of features and principles. Poujafari and Vahidpour (2014) observe that the primary focus of this literature on marginal groups brings it under postcolonial theory. Post-colonialism in its most recent definition is concerned with persons from groups outside the dominant groups and therefore places subaltern groups in a position to subvert the authority of those with hegemonic power (p. 686). Ashcroft (1995) observes that post-colonial theory entails migration, slavery, suppression, resistance, representation and influences to discourses to imperial Europe (p. 2). The theory can be applied to the topic of resistance because African literature is positioned at the margins of dominant, European literature. Taking into account the fact that post-colonial studies turn the world upside down, a study that looks at issues from the view of the despised aptly comes under it (Young, 2003, p. 2). Pertinent concepts of post colonial theory are cultural hybridity and cultural fixity.

Hall (1990) comes up with models of cultural identity that define transition of identity of the Caribbean populace. First, he postulates the traditional model that views identity in terms of one shared culture, hiding inside the many. Hall refers to it as artificial for cultural values are imposed on people because they share a history and ancestry. Citing the Caribbean example, Hall asserts that Caribbeans use this model to seek rediscovery of identity in Africa given their African origin (p. 393). He likens this to what Frantz Fanon calls "Passionate research," (ibid). Hall points out that such identity was crucial in postcolonial struggles but is not relevant in the contemporary, cosmopolitan world. Bhabha expounds on the concept of cultural fixity. He observes that fixity is a barrier to positive change. Referring to Fanon, he stresses that perpetual insistence on past traditions hinders transformation. He asserts that Fanon's metaphor that the people are in "Fluctuating movement of occult instability," is not plausible without acknowledging the third space (Bhabha, 1988, p. 207).

Bhabha (1994) observes that sticking to past histories and cultures would bring about dangers of fixity and fetishism of identities and it would deny the writer insight into experiences beyond the borders. He writes:

> Fanon recognizes the crucial importance for subordinated peoples asserting their indigenous cultural traditions and retrieving their repressed histories. But he is far too aware of the dangers of fixity and fetishism of identities within the calcification of colonial cultures to recommend that roots be struck in the celebratory romance of the past by homogenizing the history of the present (p.9).

In this text, Bhabha suggests that cultural fixity is asserting past traditions and reliving repressed histories. It lauds fixed identities and denounces mixed ones. Said (1977) observes that oriental scholars laid the foundation of cultural fixity when they divided the world into two essential factions: the Orient and the Occident. They described the Occident as rational, humane, strong, and powerful as opposed to the Orient that is irrational, inhuman, weak and sexually unstable. He writes, "Europe is powerful and articulate, Asia is defeated and distant. It is Europe that articulates the Orient… the orient insinuates danger. Rationality is undermined by Eastern excesses," (57). By creation of these binary factions, orientalist scholars posited a polarity typical of cultural fixity. Orientalism is an essentializing discourse because the West sees itself as far better than the East. After independence, Africans asserted their culture leading to polarity between them and the West. Cultural fixity therefore sets the stage for conflict, which Bhabha refers to as the politics of polarity.

Bhabha postulates the concept of hybridity as a space between two essentialist groups with attributes of them both. In his work *Location of Culture*, he observes that sticking to past traditions and cultures not only leads to fixity and fetishness of identities but denies the writer insight into new experiences. Bhabha exhorts nations that were victims of colonialism to choose the third space to fit in the changing cosmopolitan world. Indeed those Blacks who have succeeded in the West like Barack Obama are metaphors of hybridity. They have deserted cultural fixity and essentialism and stood in the middle to serve the white and black race. His Muslim father and Christian mother, white mother and black mother endeared him to both races and religions.

4:3 Postcolonialism in the Novel and Drama.

Most African novelists and playwrights after independence wrote to fight colonial ideas that had been inculcated during the colonial period to demean the African culture. Examples of such writers are Ngugi wa Thiong'o, Chinua Achebe, Peter Abrahams, Meja Mwangi, Alex la Guma, and Francis Imbuga. Other writers just presented the struggle of the marginal group against the dominant groups that oppress them. These include John Ruganda in Uganda and Nuruddin Farah in Somalia. Zimbabwean authors like Petinah Gappah and Brian Chikwava depict the struggle of the minority Zimbabweans against dictatorial regime or immigrants against the dominant hosts.

4:3.1 Oppression and Madness: A Postcolonial Critique of Selected African and American Works of Fiction

> All my life's been full of hard trouble. If I wasn't hungry,
> I was sick. And I wasn't sick, I was in trouble. I just
> work hard every day as long as I can remember. Bessie (Wright,
> 1940, 269)

The above quote from the character Bessie in Richard Wright's *Native Son* demonstrates the damaging potential of oppression in destroying the psyche of the oppressed. The system encumbers the African Americans with unending toil in hostile working conditions. The consequence is incessant trauma and inability to enjoy the fruit of their labour. Many social scientists suggest that there is nexus between oppression and mental illness. The inability to resist highhanded political and administrative systems has severe psychological consequences on the subjects. This paper interrogates the connection between oppression and madness in selected African and American works. Using the postcolonial theory, it analyses oppressed characters to investigate whether their mental illnesses stem from oppression. The main texts in this study are John Ruganda's *The Burdens* (1972), Francis Imbuga's *Betrayal in the City* (1976), Richard Wright's *Native Son* (1940) and Toni Morrison's *Beloved*. The assumption behind this comparative analysis is that the repressive experience of both Africans and Afro-Americans is similar due to the underlying racial *otherness*.

Oppressive regimes and environments are prone to insanity right from family, educational institutions and political spheres. It is the nature of human persons to resist unlawful and unethical instructions, but when a repressive system uses the instruments of power to intimidate those who resist it then the subjects undergo trauma and mental disintegration. Those with the nerve to resist are most likely to do things that are inconsistent with the morals of society.

4:3.1.1 Madness

Feder (1980) defines "madness" as "a state in which unconscious processes predominate over conscious ones to the extent that they control them and determine perceptions of and responses to experience that, judged by prevailing standards of logical thought and relevant emotion, are confused and inappropriate" (5). She further argues that the variations of "madness" created in literature often reflect what human society has discovered about it. In *Madness and Modernism*, Louis Sass (1992) describes "madness" as a condition that involves decline or even disappearance of the role of reason in human conduct and experience. Defining madness, Reid (2002) asserts:

> The term 'madness' has been used the world over with a multiplicity of meanings and implications. The scale of the term ranges from mere anger and rashness to irrationality, intoxication and ecstasy to fantasy and illusion to transcendence, delusion and psychosis. Whether we consider 'madness' a physical disease, a brain dysfunction, a deluge of passion, divine intervention, possession, repression or the consequence of environmental stress, consistent in these understandings and aetiologies is the underlying concept that 'madness' entails estrangement from reality. (15)

What is evidently common in the definitions above is the implication that "madness" is a deviation from rational reality of the societal norm; basically, it is something undesirable. Madness, can be perceived as a nebulous, non-medical term that has subjective meaning, very different from scientifically defined "insanity" or "mental illness. Feder (1980) observes:

> [...] literary interpretations of madness both reflect and question medical, cultural, political, religious, and psychological assumptions of their time[...] they explore the very processes of symbolic transformation of these influences and disclose their psychic consequences in the minds of individual characters or personae (4).

This quote interprets madness as a reaction that was exhibited by the colonized in the postcolonial period both in Africa and America. Taking a cue from Feder, it establishes that madness was a psychological response to colonization. All the authors in the selected fiction demonstrate that otherness and oppression destabilize the African and American subjects and psychic collapse is the consequence. The assumption in this chapter is that madness is a conscious or unconscious psychic response to oppressive circumstances that prevail around an individual. Through it however, the oppressed can realize who they are and in so doing, they can chart their own path to success.

4:3.1.2 Of Alcoholism and Madness in Ruganda's *The Burdens*

The play is set in the post colonial Uganda. The playwright depicts a turbulent society through the family of Wamala. Wamala, the protagonist and a former teacher lives in a façade. This is after he rose from a teacher to the position of minister in government. As a minister he could enjoy all the privileges associated with it. Reliving the past, Wamala is unable to live the present because of the biting poverty that embroils his family. His wife (Tinka) weaves mats to eke a living since there is no alternative. In addition, he is not able to provide school fees for Kaija, proper medication for Nyakake and pay poll tax. He feels humiliated as he loses the trust of his family. His madness is portrayed when he resorts to drinking and adultery in order to escape the reality. Supriya (1995) observes, "[w]hen madness was identified as a female malady [...] men were marked as idiots and drunks 'higher' upon the scale of social deviance" (p.132). Wamala's alcoholism and adultery fuel antagonism with his wife. This deviant behaviour culminates to his death. In a dream, Kaija sees his father's death in "[b]ut then...I saw you and father tearing at each other like mud... in that pool" (p.72). Kaija construes the domestic squabble between his father and mother as craziness.

Wamala madness is also evident when he is easily cheated by the Yankees (foreigners) that he could make a good president. Reid (2002) refers to this as "ecstasy to fantasy and illusion" (15), as he exalts in even without consideration that it never was his ambition. It is irrational for Wamala to resolve so rashly to challenge the president just because the Yankees have proposed it. Reid identifies "rashness" as a form of insanity. Wamala was then an executive minister of local government. He says, "[i]t was these Yankees and their dollars. Said I could make a better boss" (p.43). Because Wamala rashly believed in the Yankees, he lost his job as a minister and charged with treason. He was jailed for two years. He was also lucky not to have faced the firing squad. The mere mention of being better boss does not justify Wamala's treason charges; punishment is not in tandem with the crime committed. The "firing squad" symbolises an oppressive regime that murders suspects over trivia. Wamala leaves jail and is relegated to a hand to mouth existence. By scaling down the ladder from a minister to a pauper, Wamala is able to experience what a common man feels. He is discriminated against in employment opportunities to seal his frustration. The heat of oppression is pathological and his psyche starts disintegrating. His sole means of resistance is "reactionary psychosis" (Fanon, 1963, p.251). This can be adduced from the play:

> Wamala: The board said I was a nut and reactionary, he told me. That I can't operate in the new political spirit. Can you imagine? A nut and reactionary, and my fifty quid gone crying in his throat.
> Tinka: What is the trick now?
> Wamala: A mighty rage vibrated through me. It was hard controlling myself. I could have strangled the cheat. I simply walked away to the Republic Park and did a great deal of thinking. Real concentrated thinking. (p.20)

Wamala is disappointed when he bribes in order to get a job. He loses his meagre fifty shillings, but the board disqualifies him because of being sceptical of the oppressive regime. He almost strangled the person that he corrupted. This reaction is reasonable in Fanon's perspective because the oppressed saves himself by resisting the oppressor. He writes:

> Colonialism is a systematised negation of the other, a frenzied attempt to deny the other any attribute of humanity…which if left unchallenged by armed resistance, the colonized's defenses collapse and many of them end up in psychiatric institutions (182).

Had Wamala left the oppression unchallenged, he would have undergone total psychical collapse. His challenge to the oppressor leaves him with reactionary psychosis, which is a temporary form of insanity. He goes to the bar and begins to think in order to wallow out of his miserable state. This temporary insanity enables Wamala to reconstruct himself. He comes up with the idea of two tops for a matchstick instead of one. Wamala's new idea is what Reid will specify as a type of madness called "intoxication and ecstasy to fantasy" (15). It is irrational because two tops on a matchstick will not just make it cumbersome but also wasteful because the remaining stick after the first lighting will be dirty and too small. The user may dispose the matchstick. He wants to sell the idea to the Safety Matches. Because he is poor, his idea does not see the light of day. It is dismissed by the rich as represented by Vincent Kanagonago who purports to be one of the directors in the company.

Vincent mannerisms depict how the ruling class persecutes the poor. They have aped the whites. Vincent is depicted as callous and pompous. He is out to become rich at the expense of the poor. Wamala says:

> I'll tell you, my girl. This is luxury. The opium of the bourgeoisie. Big business, big mansions, big-bottomed wives. An endless search for extras that one doesn't really need. That is luxury. The cornerstone of exploitation. (Heating up:) Why in the devil's name can't they put chemical heads on both ends of the stick? (Ruganda, 1970, p.23)

Wamala castigates the rich for not being themselves. They want to amass wealth and live like the bourgeoisie. This is the rationale behind the exploitation that is meted on the poor. He feels that by having two chemical heads on a match stick, the poor can be relieved. However, the Vincents of the ruling class have segregated the poor in the development agenda of the country. A mad Wamala picks a fight with Vincent, when he rubbishes his idea of the matches. He strangles him. Reid considers these anger outburst and brawls as madness because reason guards against all forms of misconduct in the public domain. Vincent is saved by the police. This is after warning Vincent that the pauper that he is spitting at is being bled by black vipers like him. A day will come when they will feel the strain (p.60). As he threateningly advances towards him, he cautions him that "[o]ne day shriveled fingers will throttle fat throats..." (p.61). Drawing from Saakana (1987) "psychological programming was responsible for the schizophrenic attitudes, neurosis, mental trauma, and double consciousness of the Caribbean writer" (p.102). The mental trauma that Wamala undergoes is from the oppressor (black viper). It has made him reactionary. It is out of it that he realizes himself.

It is evident from the dissection of *The Burdens* that an oppressive environment exposes people to madness. Papanek (1994) observes that when states or other powerful institutions (such as political movements, social groups like castes or clans or domestic groups) [...] effectively limit identity choices by enforcing conformity to norms or ideals, individual freedom of action declines (p.42). Oppressors (states) employ state machinery like the police (firing squad) to scare and gag the mouths of those who are reactionary. If the oppressed partly challenge the oppressor, they suffer temporary insanity and reactionary psychosis (like Wamala), but if they do not resist at all, they completely run mad.

4:3.1.3 Powerlessness and Insanity in Imbuga's *Betrayal in the City*

The play is an indictment of dictatorial regimes that thrive on foreign aid and oppressing the masses. Ngugi wa Thiongo in his introduction to Saakana's (1987) book avers that colonialism destroys Africa's culture and replaces it with foreign culture (p.10). In his other works like *The Devil on the Cross,* he suggests that independence in African states replaced white colonialists with black ones to perpetuate the oppression of people.

This is evident in Francis Imbuga's *Betrayal in the City* as Boss, the villain in the play, rules Kafira with an iron hand. There are arbitrary arrests, no rule of law, no parliament; rules are made anyhow and executed. Boss has a kitchen cabinet comprised of the semi illiterate cousin, Mulili. They help him to make irrational decisions that oppress the people of Kafira. In order for the colonized to be free and mentally healthy, they have to resist or react to oppression. When university students organize a peaceful demonstration to protest against the influx of foreign expatriates in Kafira, Boss directs the police to use force to quell the demonstration. Adika, their leader, gunned down in the streets.

His brother, Jusper is embittered by the demise of Adika, but is so powerless to fight against the system. It hurts to learn that his brother's murderer, Chagaga, is free and roaming the village after committing a capital offence confounds him. Jusper starts experiencing mental disintegration. His speech comprises of prattles:

> Jupiter, absent sir
> Justice, absent sir
> Squad! Attention! Tututututu! (p. 4).

At this instance, Jusper is in what Reid refers to as "ecstasy to fantasy" (p. 15), since he imagines what he will do if given chance to possess a weapon. His anger is unschooled, which too in Reid's terms is madness. He single handily hunts down Chagaga and kills him to avenge his brother's death. When he returns, he announces that he has killed Chagaga, the very summit of irrationality. The crowd assembles and stones him, but he has sent his message: whoever takes someone's life should lose his too. Like Mukhtaar in Nuruddin Farah's *Close Sesame*, madness is a strategy of resistance against oppressive regimes.

Jusper tells the audience, "People say I am mad. My own mother thinks I am out of my mind. But that, (...) that when I show them will prove I have sense here" (p.5). Jusper is apprehended and detained. The government retaliates by killing his parents, Doga and Nina and releases him to return to nothing. Jusper vows to revenge the death of his parents, an insanity that pervades Kafira where the rule of the jungle is law. Juper's dressing has a lot to desire. Regina complains of his shabbiness in a red coat, which he wears to signify the fight for liberation. In a conversation with Tumbo, he reveals that there is no beer he has not tasted (41). Jusper too is creative writer; he writes plays but has never published because "his truth is too much in the nude" (p. 47). His creative genius is a symptomatic of insanity. Chigwedere asserts that "creative processes are accomplished through the crossing of the fine line between rational and irrational thinking" (p. 33), and concludes that there is very fine line between creativity and genius.

Stenberg (2001) defines creativity as the potential to create novel products that are appropriate and high quality. Christine Battersby (1989) describes a genius as one who has "instinct, emotion, sensibility, intuition and imagination" (p.10), and Kristeva (2001) suggests that "madness" is "a formidable transitory state, a tireless source of creativity" (p. 8). Using a fine written play and ingenuously directed, Jusper accomplishes his goal as revolutionary by overthrowing Boss and killing Mulili the embodiment of oppression that has pervaded Kafira all along. Mulili brags to be Boss's 'eye' and 'ear' (p.13), and taken advantage of this to murder Jusper's parents, assassinate his colleague, Kabito, in a fake road accident and betrayed Boss himself.

Through Mosese, we realize the extent of the oppression in Kafira. During Adika's burial, the government issues impromptu rules that infringe on the fundamental rights and freedoms of the citizens.

"The service must not take more than ten minutes. The coffin should not be carried by students. Weeping in public is illegal for the academic staff. I couldn't bear it, so I told them my mind" (p. 25). Mosese, Adika's lecturer, stands and opposes the oppressive rules. For Fanon this is reactionary psychosis, which challenges oppression and saves the subject's psyche. The dictatorial regime plants illegal drugs on him and have him charged with possession of illegal drugs. Mosese's incarceration renders him powerless and his psyche collapses. When Jere shares his cell, he is confounded with Mosese's mental health. First, he overreacts and grabs Jere's throat just because he says "sorry" after Mosese recounts the incident of his sister's torture. At night, he wakes up and starts walking in a nightmare. He greets people and gives a speech: "I will take up the new job… such struggles call for sacrifice [...] I will one day marry," (p. 30-31). In this sleep walking experience, we learn that he has a mental problem, and also, he has never got married at his age. His initial refusal to participate in the play is Laing's concept of the embodied self, which is too alienated from reality that it can only criticize (p. 74). With much engagement from the understanding Jere, Mosese accepts to participate in the play that has been authored by Jusper. Through it, Jere, Mosese and Jusper will come face to face with the oppressor (Boss). This action makes Boss ashamed of his wrong doing. Through Jere, it is clear that change cannot be realized through the lunatic "wait and see" attitude of Mosese. The persecutor must be challenged as Wamala does to Vincent Kanagonago in *The Burdens*. Szasz (1971) argues "[w]hat is called 'mental illness' (or 'psychopathology') emerges as the name of the product of a particular kind of relationship between oppressor and oppressed" (p.81).

Williams (1998) observes "[a]lternative views of madness and mental illness suggest that mental illness labelling has been used as an attempt to control and suppress certain members of the society" (p.14). This is what happens to Mosese, Jere, Jusper and other prisoners in Kafira. They are relegated as lunatics, for instance when the Askari tells Jere, "My God, this is the wrong place for you. The place for lunatics is three doors down the corridor" (p.16). The Askari warns Jere that if he cannot be silent like Mosese in the cell, he may land in the maniacs' prison. This is meant to repress him. However, it is through realizing who they are that Jere, Mosese and Jusper liberate Kafira.

4:3.1.4 Of Racial *Otherness* and Madness: Examination of Wright's *Native Son*

In *Native Son,* Richard Wright depicts racial oppression of the Afro-Americans and its psychological effects on them. The state security does not concern itself with the security of the black people and so, Bigger Thomas and fellow gangsters find it convenient to rob black Americans (p. 52). As appertains to accommodation, African Americans can only get accommodated in Black Belt, which is overcrowded. Bigger, his mother, Buddy and their sister, Vera. The whites live in posh areas with enough space. During his flight, Bigger enters an unoccupied building that in a white Estate. Through the window, he sees an African American with a family of four sleeping in a single room. Narrator says:

> There were quick, jerky movements on the bed where the man and the woman lay and three children were watching... five of them sleeping in one room and here is an empty building with just me in it. (p. 286)

The African Americans stay in very old houses because the rental agencies claim there are no enough houses for "Negroes". Biggers parents move out of house which collapses two days later. In payment of rents, African Americans pay twice as much as the whites for the same kind of flats (288).

African Americans are not just segregated on the job market, their work conditions are terrible. Bigger says that those who join the army dig ditches, wash dishes and scrub floors because of their race. The system allots them menial jobs and overworks them. Bessie, Bigger's girlfriend, has worked in white kitchens all her life under recriminations and commands. She tells Bigger: "Please, all I do is work, work like a dog. From morning to night I aint got no happiness" (p. 219). The high unemployment rate among the blacks compels Bigger to survive by robbery and violence. Before her death, Bessie tells Bigger:

> All my life's been full of hard trouble. If I wasn't hungry,
> I was sick. And I wasn't sick, I was in trouble. I just
> work hard every day as long as I can remember. (p. 269)

Bessie represents the oppressed African American community in the United States who slave for the Whiteman all their lives and the only reward is sickness or insanity. They have no time to reflect about their predicament. In social relations and interactions, African Americans are prohibited form shaking the hand of the white people. Bigger refuses to shake Jan's hand. African Americans have to address a white man as "Yes Sir" and white woman, "Yes Madam". When Jan refuses the formalities, Bigger is tongue-tied. Romantic relationships between black men and white women are forbidden. Bigger Thomas is so scared of Mary Dalton when she invades his private space in the car. Bigger says, "[a]ll I knew was that they kill us for women like her…we live apart" (p. 388). While grilling Jan, Bucklery ask, "[d]id you advise miss Dalton to have sexual relations with him? […] did you shake hands with that Negro?" (357- 358). The narrator says that to confess that one had committed a sex crime of that nature was to invite a death sentence (p. 282).

African Americans are stigmatized. The whites describe the African Americans as ugly, for instance, Bigger is said to "[l]ook exactly like an ape" (p. 317). They are also tagged, rapists. Since they are ugly, the whites assume that the black men always lust after white girls. They say of Bigger, "Imagine how this man overpowered Mary, raped her, murdered her." (p. 318). But when we turn to that tragic night, both Bigger and Mary were drunk and she responded well to his advances. African Americans are tagged as murderers. His lawyer, Max says, "[w]hat does matter is that he was guilty before he killed" (p. 436).

These oppressive circumstances turn Afro Americans to neurotics. There is extreme fear in Bigger's person for white people such that he has to walk with a gun to feel safe. When he goes to rob Mr Blums, a white man, he gets so scared until his colleague Gus realises it. When asks him, Bigger fights him and the plan fails. The narrator says, "Bigger was afraid of robbing a white man and he knew Gus was afraid too" (p. 63). When he visits the Daltons the first day, he can hardly speak out of fear: "Er... er...I want to see Mr Dalton". Unknown to the Daltons, he is carrying a gun. He justifies this by saying, "[h]e was going among white people so he would take his knife and gun, it would make him feel he was equal to them," (p. 81). The fear in Bigger's person has in him ingrained psychological problems. He is mad as illustrated by such unreasonable arguments. While talking to Miss Peggy, he avoids eye contact because she is a white woman. As she stares at him, Bigger looks away in confusion (p. 84). His relationship with Jan and Mary the first on job, demonstrates psychological anomalies. He misconstrues Mary's kind spirit, and even Max later reminds him that Mary was just being kind to him. When

Mary talks to him freely in Dalton's presence, Bigger mentally says, "[w]hy did she have to do this when he was trying to get a job" (p. 91). Bigger fears that her interest in him will provoke Dalton to deny him the job. After he is informed that he will earn twenty five dollars in a week, he retreats to his internal monologue and says, "This was not going to be a bad job, the only thing bad so far was the crazy girl" (p. 93). Why would Bigger behave contrary to our expectations? Will a young man not rejoice to be appreciated by a beautiful young lady? Chigwedere refers to this deviation from the norm as madness.

Bigger's condition is well summarised in Fanon's concept of abandonment neurosis. He observes that children who have submitted to familial authority whether from Africa or Europe have potential to submit to the authority of any other state in the world. However, the contrary is the case among black people. He writes, "[w]e observe the opposite in the man of colour. A normal negro child having grown up within a normal family will become abnormal on the slightest contact with the white world," (Fanon, 2008, 140). Bigger's ego collapses whenever he meets white people because of the fear they have inculcated in him for generations. He sees white people as a "force" instead of human persons. That is why Mary's tendency to lean on his shoulder on the way home devastates rather than edify him. He says, "[s]he made me feel like a dog... I was mad...I wanted to cry (p. 405). Bigger drives Mary back home and worriedly lead her to the bedroom. He gets tempted to have her and hardly have they made love when her blind mother gropes in. The white phobia seizes him and with all his strength puts his hand on Mary's mouth to stop her from speaking. In a transport of fear, he dodges Mrs Dalton's hands while pressing Mary deeper into the pillow case. When Mrs Dalton leaves the room, Bigger is confounded to see the lifeless body of Mary. He tells Max later, "[h]onest to God, I didn't know what I was doing. It was like another man stepped into my skin and started acting for me". In court, max says, Bigger has "poor mental and emotional attitude, (408). In short, Bigger is insane owing to the racial oppression he has experienced since childhood. Like all other schizoids, Bigger has crazy ideas. He tells Max:

> Maybe this sounds crazy. Maybe they are going to burn me in electric chair for feeling this way. But I aint worried none about women I killed. For a little while I was free. I was doing something. I was wrong, but I was feeling alright. [...] I wanted to do things, but everything I wanted to do, but all I wanted to do I couldn't. (p. 392)

Bigger's madness is a kind of desperation created by racial oppression. He implies that the whites relegate the Afro Americans in noble tasks of nation building and the only field left for the oppressed is negative self actualization. The sole available means for fame and self realization is murder and robbery, which is madness.

4:3.1.5 Of Slavery and Madness: Critique of Morrison's *Beloved*

This postcolonial novel rekindles the memories of 1860s after the American civil war. It retells the trauma that those who escaped from slavery had to grapple with. In a moving account, Sethe, the protagonist narrates the dehumanizing oppression of the black slaves under the hands of the salve masters. She is an escapee of slavery from Sweet Home where she lived with her daughter, Denver, in Cincinnati 124 Bluestone road. This is after she had killed her daughter in it. This can be adduced in "[f]ull of a baby's venom. The women in the house knew it and so did the children" (p.3). This happened when Schoolteacher, his previous master at Sweet Home came to recapture them. Because of the oppression that Sethe went through as a slave, she resolves to kill her children rather than allow them become slaves.

Women slaves were "cows" to reproduce more slaves. Sethe's mother-in law baby Suggs had eight children with six fathers, just as cows do. Narrators says, "[h]er two girls, neither of whom had their adult teeth were sold and gone and had not been able to wave good bye," (p. 29). Slavery denies her dignity of proper family life. Sethe is a mere breeder at Mr Garner's house and school teacher cherishes her fertility. He was elated because his four children were being raised to be taken back to "Kentucky, raise property, to do work that Sweet Home desperately needed," and he was happy because Sethe had "ten breeding years left" (p. 184). Sethe knew the plight of a fellow female slaves in the hands of white men. Ella, for instance is locked up in the room for a full year to satiate sexual feelings of a white father and his son (146), and as if this did not suffice, her mother-in-law, Baby Suggs had to have sex with the white master to keep her third child with her (p. 29); however, he was traded for lumber and found herself pregnant by the master who had promised not to sell the boy. School teacher takes Sethe to a stable, strips her, has her milked and raped before her husband, Haile. Sethe says, "They took my milk and he saw it and didn't come... if he is alive and saw that, he won't step foot in my door. Not Halle" (p. 85).

Female slaves like Sethe and Baby Suggs were sometimes forced to sleep with their sons. Baby Suggs is happy with the garner's type of slavery since he did not "bring her sons to her cabin with orders to lay with her like they did in Carolina" (p. 173).

These and many other oppressive practices lead to psychic collapse among slaves in Morrison's *Beloved*. The male slave Haille, sees white men strip his wife, milk her and rape her before his very eyes. His inability to challenge the ordeal destroys his psyche and runs mad on the spot. It is embarrassing that the so called protector of the family is so demascularized by the slave master that he can do nothing to protect his family. At Sweet Home, male slaves are denied their manhood and turn to insane acts of sex like bestiality. Morrison writes, "[m]en are all in their twenties, minus women, fucking cows, dreaming of rape... they were young and so sick of the absence of women" (p. 31). When Sixo meets a young man and makes advances, the white man gets them and have him punished. After Mr. Garner's death, the men slaves flee Sweet Home, but School master intercepts them and kills Sixo. Paul D is beaten and brought back. The pain he has experienced traumatizes his self and he undergoes alienation. At one point he cannot tell whether the screaming he hears is his own or someone else's. Sometimes he is insecure; so much so that he wonders whether he is a real man. Having seen Aunt Phylis run mad, Sethe fears that he could end up insane, but her crazy decision to express her love for her children by butchering them confirms her insanity. The magnitude of oppression of slavery drives her motherly nature to reach the decision that the best expression of love is murder of her children. She had looked forward to a free life, a happy life in the north. When School teacher gets her braced to take her back to the squalid life, the dream is shattered. She decides to kill her children and by the time she is stopped, beloved, her third child is dead.

Beloved's return as a ghost represents the trauma caused by slavery, which disturbs the mind of African Americans today. It was a destructive and painful past that haunts the present generation of black Americans. Morrison wonders how the whites expect African American to be mentally sound when they know their fathers were assaulted and sold like bulls. How would it be business as usual when their mothers were milked like cows? For, Bailey (1942), the trauma results in complicated psychological anomalies like split personality.

4:3.1.6 Conclusion

In conclusion, there is a nexus between diverse forms of oppression and madness; it is a reactionary behaviour by the oppressed towards oppressor. Postcolonial situation in this subsection is evident in the contest between the dominant group (the oppressor) and the marginal group (the oppressed). The insanity is manifested via queer straits like alcoholism, sexual perversion, violence, fear and murder as related in the dissection of the selected texts. From Africa to America, it has been established that the experience of imperialism had a deleterious impact on the psyche of the colonized. Madness had a curative as well as a degenerative function to their minds. Despite this, it was the only way that the blacks had to realize themselves and map their own destiny.

4:3.2 The In-between Space- Alienation and Psychological Trauma: A Postcolonial Critique of Jean Rhys' *Wide Sargasso Sea* and Velma Pollard's *Homestretch*.

The focus of this subsection is examination of in-between hybrid identity and the consequent alienation on marginal groups with close reference to Rhy's novel *Wide Sargasso Sea* and Pollard's *Homestretch*. Minorities that live in alien cultures choose hybridity as strategy of resistance against discrimination. Although it is an effective strategy of coexistence, young migrant characters experience alarming levels of psychological instability. Erikson (1968) observes that adolescents who migrate during years of "identity crisis" (p.220) to foreign countries experience complicated cultural transition marked by ambivalence and identity split. As a result, these children attempt to incorporate *here* and *there* into a meaningful sense of *self*. The constant shift from one end of the identity continuum to the other in young migrant characters causes internal fragmentation that may lead to insanity.

Depression, stroke and madness are recurring motifs in migration literature owing to tendency of characters to choose the in-between space. Older migrant characters are comparatively stable in spite of facing same discriminatory experiences like youthful immigrants. In this subsection, the author analyses levels of hybridity and their effect on the inner life of migrant characters. Using Homi Bhabha's concept of hybridity the subsection explores the impact of in-between hybrid identity on the mental health of characters in Jean Rhys' *Wide Sargasso Sea* and Velma Pollard's *Homestretch*.

Minority communities at the margin of dominant majorities in foreign communities experience a lot of discrimination and some choose the middle ground to negotiate their existence in the alien environment. To elude the possibility of polarity and violence, minority groups choose the middle ground to coexist with the dominant group. The hybrid space however comes with negative psychological effects on the migrant characters.

Bhabha (1994) defines hybridity as the ambivalent site where attributes of two essential groups are synthesized. He refers to hybrid identities as "in-between" identities, defined as identities in which humans are not "this or that" but are both "this or that" and neither "this and that". He stresses that hybridity is "a constant state of contestation and flux caused by differential systems [...] the unstable element of linkage" (p.227). At one point they behave like white characters and other times like black characters thereby vacillating on the identity continuum, which results in psychological problems. Let us now examine Rhys' and Pollard's characters under the microscope of hybridity.

4:3.2.1 In- between Identities in Rhys' *Wide Sargasso Sea* and Pollard's *Homestretch*.

In his thesis on construction of identity among Kurdish immigrants in Sweden, Sulyman A (2014) implies that there are three levels of hybrid identities: *Shared sense, in-between, Western skewed and More ethnic hybrid identities*. Some Kurdish immigrants exhibit *shared sense* hybridity in that they appreciate both Kurdish and Swedish culture in equal measure while others are more inclined towards Kurdish culture hence referred to as *More ethnic* hybrid identities. Sulyman suggests that *In-between* identities are those immigrants who vacillate between the culture of host community and that of their countries of origin. He comes across a Kurdish immigrant, Shilan, who having migrated to Sweden at the age of six months sometimes feels "full Kurd" and other times "in- between" and other times just "different" (p. 28-29). In *Wide Sargasso Sea* and *Homestretch*, there are migrant characters that depict the various levels of hybridity, and those with the in-between hybrid identity experience alienation and psychological trauma.

Set at Coulibri Estate in the Caribbean after the Emancipation Act, Jean Rhys' *Wide Sargasso Sea* is a moving novel about the plight of black minority groups in white dominant majorities in the Caribbean. After the end of slavery in 1833, the freed slaves underwent harrowing experiences in the Caribbean. The relations between the white slave owners and black slaves resulted in half caste children with a double identity who found it difficult to fit in the highly polarized society; as a result, they suffered from heightened levels of ambivalence. To the blacks these children were repulsed because they were not black enough. To the whites, they were repulsed because they were not white. The result was profound pain, anguish, and deep-seated fragmentation that drove some to psychological distress and madness. The same condition dominates Velma Pollard's *Homestretch*. Characters that emigrate from Caribbean to England and Americas after the Second World War experience a cultural clash and in their attempt to negotiate their existence get tremendously alienated. The rootlessness and lack of a sense of belonging in a culturally hostile environment causes far-reaching psychological problems. These psychological problems are consequence of anomalies in the identity formation process which demands that ethnic identity precede hybridity for stable personality development (Jaspal and Cinnirrella, 510). The in-between hybrid identity bypasses ethnic identity to cast the young characters in an ambivalent space: the arena of rootless fluidity and unending struggle in search for identity.

Rhys' *Wide Sargasso Sea* and Pollard's *Homestretch* depict the struggle of minority black groups at the margins of a dominant white society undoubtedly bringing the texts under the postcolonial criticism. In the two novels, the novelists depict migration, slavery, suppression and resistance, which are pertinent to post-colonial criticism. In *Wide Sargasso Sea,* characters like Antoinette choose the hybrid space to resist discrimination with no vestige of success. In *Homestretch,* migrant characters such as Brenda, choose the in-between identity to negotiate their existence in England and United States with varying degrees of success.

The principal characters to be used in this subchapter are Antoinette, Annette, Daniel Cosway and Rochester in *Wide Sagasso Sea* and David, Brenda and Laura in *Homestretch.* Antoinette, born of a white father and Mulatto mother, is the heroine in Rhys' *Wide Sargasso Sea.* Pitted against black racism and white racism, Antoinette undergoes intense internal fragmentation resulting in the loss of sanity. Annette is Antoinette's mother who is hated by black people in Coulibri Estate for marrying Cosway, a slave owner. Soon after her husbands demise, the black, free slaves turn hostile against Annette. Daniel Cosway is Antoinette's step brother, born out of Cosway's affair with a black slave woman. His failure to reconcile with his father's brutality and hostility of the black race devastates his mental health. David is the hero in Pollard's *Homestretch*. He migrates from Jamaica to England after independence during the *S.S Windrush* of 1948 to heed the call of rebuilding the Mother Land after the Second World War (Lau, 2). Laura is David's niece that migrates to England for further education and returns to work in Jamaica. Brenda is Laura's friend; she meets in England in one of her lectures. Brenda goes to the United States to live with her father and later migrates to England when her father gets married to a British nurse. The study focuses on the manner in which these characters employ hybridity to negotiate their existence in the maze of cultures and how it impacts on their inner life.

4:3.2.2 The In-between World and Alienation

While investigating ambivalence among adolescent immigrants in the diaspora, Zubida H. et al (2014) remark that immigrant children face conflicting social contexts in which they attempt to incorporate "here" and "there" into meaningful sense of the "self". Citing Portes & Rubiin (2005), they write:

> Among adolescent immigrants, this process is more complex and often entails the juggling of competing allegiances and attachments. Situated within two cultural worlds, they must define themselves in relation to multiple reference groups (sometimes in two countries and languages) and the classifications in which they are placed by their native peers, schools, the ethnic community and larger society. (P. 304)

Pollard's and Rhys' characters find themselves in two cultural worlds and struggle to identify themselves with the two Worlds. Brenda, having arrived from Jamaica to the United States finds the education systems of the two countries very different. Although she had maintained a brilliant academic record in Jamaica, the American teacher said "she could make no sense of the reports from home," (p.59). Her love for American education underscores her appreciation of Western values. Her mother insisted that she had to get good education from America. The glaring differences between Jamaican education and repulsion from the West are a clash Brenda has to reconcile with to coexist. The American tutors hold a contemptuous or rather spiteful attitude towards Caribbean migrant children, for instance the teacher counselor "wanted to know everything about her life, from how many grandmothers she had to how she felt about her stepmother" (p. 59). Brenda is subjected to Placement Tests and Diagnostic Tests and taken to a lower class than the one she had been in Jamaica. In the class, her learning is interrupted by occasional transfer to the home school to interact "with West Indian children," (p. 59) for psychological adjustment. With her previous detest for American tutors, we expect Brenda to like the home school due to its composition- Caribbean children. On the contrary, she perceives the decision to send her to the home school as discrimination and is unsettled by depression. In Brenda, vacillation between love for Jamaican and American culture is observed; an attribute that is typical of the in-between world. When Mrs. Saul, a visiting teacher from Jamaica, visits the school, Brenda's love for the mother country reasserts itself. The writer says, "Brenda didn't know that she was homesick. She was glad to hear the woman's voice and felt she was going to cry," (p. 60). With Mrs. Saul, she experiences a strong sense of belonging and intimacy to signify her connection with Jamaica. She opens up to her but starts complaining about the home school, the supposed source of psychological connection to the motherland with children of Caribbean origin. "She was wasting time with the group in the home room," (p. 61), Brenda said, and asked Mrs. Saul to talk to the American tutors to place her permanently in the ninth class. The reader is left to wonder to which identity Brenda belongs. At one point, she misses Jamaica and the next moment she craves American education; hence is the nature of in-between or ambivalent identities. The fluctuation of the migrant characters on the identity continuum causes alienation, defined by Encyclopaedia Britannica as "a state of feeling estranged or separated from one's milieu of work, products or self". Finkelstein (1965) defines alienation as a psychological phenomenon, "an internal conflict, a hostility felt towards something seemingly outside oneself, which is linked to oneself, a barrier erected which is actually no defense but an impoverishment of oneself," (p. 7). Finkelstein is making a reference to internal fragmentation, which is reiterated by Erich Fromm who observes, "[t]he meaning of alienation is that process of feeling in which anyone feels estranged from self," (p. 10). The in-between space that Brenda occupies upon arrival in the United States is the beginning of an internal conflict that causes inner turmoil in the greater part of the story.

In England, Brenda finds herself terribly isolated and internally fragmented. She was always lonely and never had one positive word for England. Pollard (1994) writes:

> Apart from being new, she had two strokes against her. She was black and she spoke English with an American accent. She felt that the teachers did not like her, that they were prejudiced in spite of their smiling. And the students, the black ones who were mostly Jamaican, didn't want to talk to her much. Perhaps her shyness and insecurity came over to them as stand-offishness. If they had let

her into their little groups, they would have found that nothing was wrong with her. (p. 75)

In this passage Pollard illustrates an instance of the in-between identity, which as Bhabha observes is characterized by instability: neither "this" nor "that" (227). Brenda neither likes the Jamaican students nor British teachers owing to her internal fragmentation. Her exposure to a mosaic of cultures in the United States has ruined her ethnic identity formation which would have contributed to her psychological stability. Brenda feels more isolated and "buries herself in books" (76). Finkelstein refers to this as "estrangement from the self", a personal reaction to the segregation she confronts in England. She tells Laura that she detests the hypocrisy of the English teachers, citing that they are the kind that will "shake your hand go and wash afterwards" (p. 77). The inner turmoil, emptiness and psychological trauma compel her to join a radical group in the FE College in England. Laura observes that "she was in full African Regalia and allowed her hair to go dread" (p. 79). It is after an intimate friendship with Laura that Brenda leaves the group to symbolize a reconnection to her ethnic identity and end to alienation. Citing Albert Camus, Abdul Saleem sums up the fate of immigrant characters as a lost people: "[c]ut off from his religious, metaphysical and transcendental roots, man is lost; all his actions become senseless, absurd and useless (p. 21). Brenda is uprooted from her mother culture, Jamaica and does not know who she is. Her decision to join a radical poetry group in England is an unconscious search for her roots in order to find meaning in life. But even when she comes in contact with Jamaica, she shows elements of instability, vacillating from a dislike to a liking for her. On one hand, Brenda loves Jamaican food, and tells Laura that she likes "Potato pudding" (p. 87), and loves her mother so much that she is building her a flat in Kingston. On the other hand, she prefers the English work habits (p. 88), and European clean cities: "Scandinavian cities are notoriously clean," (53), she says after arrival at Kingston. Brenda is unnerved by the tendency of the Jamaican taxi driver to flout traffic rules, something that could hardly occur in the West. Brenda's oscillation between the love and dislike for Jamaica and the West is quite eccentric. While conversing with Laura, she observes that Jamaican teachers are more dedicated than American teachers because they labour with meager pay to prepare students for performances and in the next utterance describes it as "disorganized compared to England and America" (p. 88). She then plunges in an emotional tantrum saying "is a feeling deep down that it (Jamaica) rejected me" (ibid) and gave me England.

David, like Brenda undergoes a harrowing experience in England as a result of discrimination by the dominant white majority. Upon return to Jamaica, he tells people, "[t]he white people are not easy. You have a hell of time to live with them and still remember that you are a person" (p. 20). He reveals that the West Indians living in England are not treated like human beings at the work place. David could teach the white workers practical skills in the factory but when they met outside, they could not greet him (p. 31). The racial discrimination and pressures at the work place caused them deep seated emotional wounds such that they never enjoyed their marriage. In a flashback, David says, "[s]omehow, now, he felt that he was a lone. Inside. Somewhere, somehow, they had lost it. Whatever it was," (p. 7). Unlike Brenda who vacillates between love and dislike for England, David categorically dislikes England and prefers Jamaica. Whereas the young migrant characters experience terrible psychological problems, David does not. The Jamaican villagers observe that people who go to England return when mad (p. 20). They give the example of Avis, Miss Betty's daughter, and Miss Gerald's son. David remarks, "[t]he young people you mention were children when they went to England. Maybe they couldn't stand it". (p. 21). Pollard implies that young immigrants who go to foreign countries are more vulnerable to in-between identity formation because they lack an ethnic identity to be located in the foreign environment, which results into instability and psychological trauma. Jaspal & Cinnirella (2011) observe that "identification with the ethnic group (among immigrants) has positive implication" (p. 510), since identity is constructed by way of difference. Older immigrants like David and Laura leave Jamaica to England having developed an ethnic identity and therefore merely borrow a few attributes from the foreign culture to negotiate their existence. As a result, they develop an *ethnic skewed hybrid* identity that is more stable than the in-between identity among young immigrants who suffer a lot of ambivalence.

Billing (1989) observes, "[c]ommon sense contains conflicting and opposed themes or values, for instance, people should be merciful and justice should be dealt," (p. 238). Billing expounds that these conflicting situations, otherwise referred to as ambivalence, give rise to dilemmas. Rhys' characters in *Wide Sargasso Sea* exhibit ambivalence because they occupy the middle ground in a racially polarized setting. Antoinette, the prime mover in the novel, is a child of mixed parentage who struggles to adjust in racially charged community after the Emancipation Act of 1833 (Rhys, 19). She disapproves the negative reaction of the black people towards her mixed race family after the demise of her white father. All the black population around Coulibri Estate refuse to visit them and Antoinette's mother, Annette is compelled to lie to children that the road is bad. Antoinette says, "[m]y father, visitors, feeling safe, horses- all belonged to the past" (15). When Annette rides the horse around the estate, black people "stood around in groups to jeer at her especially when her clothes grew shabby" (16). Antoinette is hurt by black people after they poison their horse to death. Her choice of the word "negro" while referring to black people is evidence of her spiteful attitude towards the black race: " I never looked at any strange negro- they hated us. They called us white cockroaches," (22). One day while walking on the way, a black girl follows her singing, "[w]hite cockroaches go away…go away, nobody wants you!" (p. 23). The black community, former freed slaves, feel vindicated when Antoinette's family descends into poverty. Tia tells Antoinette, "[w]e hear all we poor like beggar… you run like calabash to catch water" (p. 23). This rejection by the two essentialist groups has a harrowing effect on Annette. The writer observes that "she talked loud to herself" (ibid) and fell in love with solitude. After the death of her idiotic son, Pierre, she ran mad and threatened to kill her second husband, Mason. The black community lays siege to their home in Coulibri, burns the home, and including the parrot. They shout, "[l]ook at the damn white niggers" (p. 30). Antoinette is stoned and bears a scar. Myra, the house maid escapes leaving Pierre behind. He dies of the injuries he sustained in the arson attack. Pierre's death alienates Annette farther from herself after she fails to accept the reality that her only son had passed on. She runs mad and threatens to kill Mason. She was confined in prison and later died. The collision between black and white cultures and the failure to reconcile the two worlds from the middle leave an incurable psychological wound on Annette's life.

After Annette's death, Mason, Antoinette's foster father, married her off to an English man. The marriage was stage managed to conceal Antoinette's "bad background". The narrator says, "[t]he Mason's family planned and married Antoinette to an Englishman who knew nothing of her background (she has bad blood of madness from both sides)," (p. 81). They hurried and did it while Rochester, the prospective husband, was ill. Readers observe different behavior in Antoinette during this marriage. Contrary to our expectation, she becomes a defender of the black ethnic group and its ways. She detests the white race, for instance, dislikes Rochester right from the engagement party. She tells Richard, Mason's son, that "she won't marry Rochester" (p. 67). But after persuasion, the marriage commences but proceeds with conflicts that are a consequence of the instability typical of in-between identities. The characters behavior in these identities depends on "social circumstances" (Cooper, 2000, 10), including the choice of words by his opponent. When Rochester looks down on St Pierre, a city in West Indies, Antoinette blurts that "it is the Paris of West Indies" (p. 67). She even hastens to add that the England and London that Rochester reveres is "a dream- a cold dark dream" (ibid) respectively. Antoinette further sympathises with Christophine, their black servant. When Rochester reprimands her for leaving her dress to flow to the ground, Antoinette tells him that black women leave their dresses to flow as a sign of respect. Despite Antoinette's earlier spite for the black race, she now trusts black people. She even "trusts black servants and gives them gifts" (p. 75), which is misconstrued by Rochester as extravagance.

With the ensuing clash of culture, Antoinette becomes a victim of rejection by her husband. When she sings songs, he blurts that her songs "only haunted him" (p. 76). As a consequence, she experiences terrible feelings of isolation or rather social-alienation. McClosky (1965) defines social alienation as "loss of significant social relationships" (p. 15) that results in harrowing psychological consequences on the person. With the lapse of time, she stops chatting with Rochester and substitutes this with conversations with Christophine in Patois. Depression gets the better of her and the husband realizes that death is the sole subject of her conversations. When he wants to know why she is never happy, she replies, "I am not used to happiness. It makes me afraid," (p. 77). Rochester's hatred for her becomes evident when he says:

> I did not love her. I was thirsty for her, but that is not love.
> I felt very little tenderness for her.
> She was a stranger to me,
> a stranger who did not think or feel as I did." (p. 78)

Rochester reveals his internal fragmentation or self alienation in a marriage bedeviled by clash of cultures. He loses his sexual feelings for her and spends his "nights in the dressing room" (p. 90). He sees his wife as a doll, devoid of any feelings. He says, "I could see Antoinette stretched on the bed quite still... like a doll" (p. 123). Christophine tries to apply Obeah methods to treat Antoinette but the psychological trauma is on the rise. Rochester is also affected by hybrid identity, though of the *ethnic skewed* type. Striving to survive among Creoles and black people at Coulibri, Rochester has more appreciation for the English culture. For example, he does not want his wife, Antoinette to kiss and hug Negroes (p. 76). In his conversation with the wife, it is clear that he detests St. Pierre and Jamaica but loves Paris and England. He tells Christophine, "I would give my eyes never to have seen this abominable place," (p. 128). Rochester's marriage to Antoinette's was a ruse hatched by his family to get rid of him from England. This symbolizes a rejection by Western culture and when he marries a woman of colour, he is rejected (by African civilization) and plunges in a state of alienation. He is estranged from the self and hence devoid of the feelings that can sustain a romantic relationship. Antoinette tells him, "[y]our mouth is colder than my hands" (p. 117). He does not miss his wife when she is away and loses his taste for the fine things of life. He says "I hate poets and poetry now, as I hate music, which I loved once" (p. 129). While talking of his harrowing experiences in England, David refers to this inner emptiness and coldness in his relationship with

Edith in *Homestretch* (p. 7). It is the result of deep seated fragmentation that results from psychological trauma from hostile cultural environment. He distrusts Antoinette's relatives and reserves no vestige of feeling for her. He says:

> However much I paid Jamaican servants
> I would never buy discretion. I would
> Be gossiped about, sung about.
> They make up songs about everybody-
> You should hear one about governor's wife. (p. 127)

Rejection of Antoinette and Rochester by the two essentialist cultures result in self alienation that has disastrous consequences on their psyche and marriage. The rootlessness causes them to oscillate between white and black but Rochester is more stable because he developed his ethnic identity in England. However, Antoinette who grew lacks an ethnic identity succumbs to the alienation and runs completely mad.

In spite of his strident criticism towards Antoinette, Daniel Cosway, exhibits symptoms of insanity. He is reckless in his treatment of his step-sister and even goes further to write a derogatory letter to Rochester with the intention of wrecking the marriage. He for instance makes the wild accusation that Antoinette had a promiscuous background because he had a boyfriend called Sandi. "You are not the first to kiss her pretty face" (p.106), he tells Rochester, which makes him doubt Daniel's sanity. He is internally fragmented because of his identity crisis. He is neither white nor black and his desire to locate his white heritage is thwarted by Old Cosway's arrogance. At sixteen, he goes to old Cosway to borrow money only to be cursed and disowned. The ensuing trauma deals a blow to Daniel Cosway and he is full of bitterness. He tells Rochester, "[t]here is a marble table in the

English church to commemorate him; I hope that stone tie around his neck and drag him down to hell in the end" (p.101). Daniel equally shares his hatred for blacks and whites leaving the reader wondering where he belongs. Old Cosway was wicked, Antoinette is promiscuous and Christophine, Rochester's black servant "the worst, she have to leave Jamaica because she go to jail," (p.103). As a result of his tattered feelings, Daniel Cosway leaves in isolation. He hates women because they are "demons incarnate who say 'buy me this, buy me that" (ibid).

4:3.2.3 Conclusion

The degree of alienation and trauma largely depends on the nature of hybrid identity chosen by the migrant character. Older characters develop the *shared sense* or *ethnic skewed* hybridity and therefore experience more psychological stability than young characters that enter the in-between space that is characterized by intense alienation and psychological instability. The missing ethnic identity that ought to have occurred in their ancestral land leaves a void that casts them in the quagmire of identity formation.

4.4 Postcolonialism and African Poetry

There are some African poets who avoided African style and chose western skewed styles of writing and were either condemned by negritude poets or ended up not having illustrious careers. One such a poet was South African Dennis Brutus who wrote in traditional Elizabethan styles without a touch of Africanness. Unlike Okot and Kofi Awoonor who wrote with images from the local African environment, Brutus wrote in European styles and metric verse, for few literary elite. Unlike the simplicity of hybrid poetry, Brutus' poetry was quite esoteric. Read the following stanza from his poem:

Postscript 2

There are of course tho' we don't see them

-I cut away the public trappings to assert

Certain private essentialities-

Some heroic aspects of this all

-People outside admire, others pity-

But it is not of these I wish to speak. (Pierce, 1990, P. 2).

Right from the title of the poem, "Postscript 2" the poem is unsuited to the ordinary, African audience. The diction alienates Brutus from the African audience and seems to lean towards the Western audience. There are many other words such as "trappings," "assert", "essentialities" that are contrary to the simplicity of African poetry. Furthermore, elements such as local imagery, repetition, direct address and direct translation that are typical of African poetry are conspicuously missing. There is a big contrast between this poem and Kofi Awoonor's stanza from the poem "Songs of Sorrow":

Dzogbese Lisa has treated me thus
It has led me among the sharps of the forest
Returning is not possible
And going forward is a great difficulty
The affairs of this world are like the chameleon feaces
Into which I have stepped

When I clean it cannot go. (Pearce, 1990, p. 49).

Awoonor stands out as a hybrid poet because he mixes elements of African poetry with Western Poetry. Although he is using English to express his concerns, he adopts features of African poetry such as images from the local environment (The affairs of this world are like the chameleon feaces), direct translation (When I clean it cannot go) and simplicity of language to show that the poem was composed in an African language and then translated into English. Aware of Brutus' indifference about hybridity, Awoonor writes a poem to reprimand him:

To Dennis Brutus

At first from your verse
The imprecise dilettante
A cocky troubadour, professional exile
Chronicler of sirens knuckles and boots
Through Texan nights
And Lousiana plains, in jazz halls
And strip joints, beneath spinning buttocks
Of dancing girls warm
A warrior without a country
A rain cloud falling on alien lands
A friend of Shakespeare, Words Worth
And the sirens of your cape. (Pearce, 1990, p. 55)

The poem begins by quoting from Brutus' own poetry having described himself in pompous tones as a cocky troubadour, and professional exile but he is seen in Texas and Louisiana dancing with licentious American girls to symbolize his love for Western culture and art. Citing Van J. & Linfor B. (2001) on Brutus' interview, Tyrone asserts that a troubadour was a composer of lyrical poetry during the middle ages in Europe (p. 28). J. H. Chaytor notes that troubadours were the first lyric poets of medieval Europe (p. 14). In the aforementioned interview, Brutus professed that he was influenced by William Shakespeare and Wordsworth and acknowledges Victorian poets such as Hopkins and Browning. This Western influence is what Awoonor refers to in this poem as a friend of Shakespeare and Wordsworth. Awoonor sums up that Brutus has no identity or place on the corpus of African literature (a warrior without a country) due to his leanings towards the Western style in writing. During his exile in the United States and China, Brutus learnt his lessons and regretted having ignored hybridity as the foundation of art in the cosmopolitan world. Tyrone notes that while in exile in China, Brutus borrowed the Chinese haiku style to write poetry to a wider audience (p. 199). He learnt that hybridity would enable him write poetry that would endear him to the ordinary person, hence a wider cosmopolitan audience. Brutus' collections such as *Poems from Algiers* and *China Poems* had simple style to exhibit the hybrid nature he had adopted later in life.

4.4.1 Cultural Hybridity in Christopher Okigbo's Poetry

Born in 1932, Okigbo was one the most talented hybrid poets whose work is steeped in mythologies of Asia, Europe and rural Igbo. Robert Fraser describes him as poet of "[w]ide and voracious reading in literatures if Greece and Rome," (p. 177). For him to be a writer was to partake in an international community of letters, not being narrowed down to Igbo culture in Nigeria. He therefore rejected what Bhabha terms as 'fixity and fetishness of identity' (9). In this connection, Okigbo turned down a prize at the first festival of black arts in Dakar, Senegal because he did not consider himself exclusively as an African writer. He did not embrace negritude because he thought it was just too simplistic. "It's not that I dislike it," he said, "it is because when you have read a lot of it, you begin to have the feeling that it is so easy to do it." Okigbo's poetry was therefore a departure from that of Okot P' Bitek and Leopold Senghor.

Okigbo constructs poems following European musical compositions in a series of movements with themes, developments, repeats and reminiscences. Sources closer to him reveal that he used to revise his works very much to shape them into a sequence. Having been a musician at Ibadan University, his constructions were heavily influenced by western musicians such as Debussy and Caesar Frank whose creative gene focuses on a nebulous world with overtones of dreams. No wonder Okigbo's poetry is very abstract and symbolic. He also uses lines from Yoruba, Igbo and Ewe praise songs to fulfill his hybrid vision. The greatest European poets that influence his works are Eliot and Ezra Pound whose poetry proceeds on dream and vision rather than narrative and drama. Let us look at some examples:

Watermaid
Bright
With the armpit dazzle of the lioness
She answers
Wearing white light about her
And the waves escort her
My lioness
Crowned with moonlight (Ulli & Gerald, 1963, 235)

The *Watermaid* depicts a dreamy moment of illumination from the water maid lioness figure; a dreamy moment for the poet coming through a sexual union. It a vision of the white goddess, a sexual union with whom generates poetry according to Robert Graves theory handed down to Okigbo by Peter Thomas. But the moment is fleeting as she leaves the poet again solitary and abandoned: "[s]he answers/ weaving white light about her/ and waves escort her/ my lioness," (p. 235).

Lustra is the title of Ezra Pounds 1916 volume of poetry, hence a Western allusion. It refers to Roman times' offerings for the sins of whole people:

> So would I to the hills again
> So would I
> To where springs the fountain
> There to draw from
> And to hilltop clamber
> Body and soul white washed in the moon dew
> There to see from
> (Ulli & Gerald, 1963, 236).

The first movement of Okigbos' Lustra is a personal ritual of cleansing and preparation. He is going to the hills where there is a shrine for cleansing. He combines it with African sacrifice of an egg and a hen: "[h]ere is a new laid egg/ have a white hen at midterm", (237). Sacrifice is another movement of Lustra where hybridity dominates. There is a Christian reference given to entirely African funeral ceremonies accompanied by 'thundering drums and canons, ceremonies recognizing continuity of earthly life with life of spirits:

> Thundering drums and canons
> In palm grove
> The spirit is in a scent
>
> I have visited

> On palm beam imprinted
> My pentagon. (Ulli & Gerald, 1963, 236)

The siren limits opens with chatter like that of a weaverbird. The tongue of the poet has been unloosed after the ritual of cleansing and sexual initiation. He is quite jaunty to the goddess now, "the queen of the damp/ half light". He impudently refers to the nude spear of Leopold Senghor of negritude and Soyinka's riposte about the tiger and tigritude.

In section two, the poet narrator listens to one of the siren's songs about himself. He is the shrub overshadowed by poplars diffident and exploratory. He needs to try on masks of the self, the various selves and relate them to his soul and his poetry. Then if he is successful, soul self and voice will cohere into a shrub that has metamorphosed into a clean cloud above the forest,

In section three, there is a climate of unreadiness. "[t]he mortar is not dry," is quoted from Ezra Pound from a letter of Sigimondo Malatesta in 1449 to mean that the plaster on the walls of his newly build chapel is not dry and so Piero cannot paint them. Here is another element of hybridity to imply that the world is not ready for his poetry.

The poet then goes through the high arched gate and follows the little stream to the lake in search of the "The big white elephant," it is an elusive creature its white skin similar to that of the white goddess. It is a demonic obsession that makes the poet become disembodied and lose his second self. Section four has him anaethetisized by his overpowering memory of sexuality of the oblong headed lioness to which he willingly yields himself up:

> Hurry down
> Through the high arched gate-

Hurry down
Little stream to the lake
Hurry down
In the wake of the dream.(Ulli & Gerald, 1963, p. 239).

Christopher Okigbo was undoubtedly a hybrid poet and one the finest poet in Africa. The subtle and abstract nature of his poetry crowns it as the best example of what poetry ought to be.

4.4.2 Modern Hybrid Poetry:

Hybrid poetry did not end with the demise of Okigbo. There are poets who strive for the hybrid space instead of the two other extremes. Let us look at the following poems:

Dual Nationality
Barry Taylor

Myself am shared by countries two,
A fever brought by both;
The hot, the cold, the blaze, the brine,
Are temperatures of truth.

The one is concerned with supple stream,
With windings like an alphabet,
An eddy's lip, a phrase, a fish
Sentences of liquid;

The other has in roaring water
Ramifying falls
A trip of rock, a clap of shine,

Crocodile and caterwaul

> The one is made of winter's war
> Snowy siege and dash of flake
> And inch by inch, in retreat
> The bugle of bird brakes
> The other seems for summer told
> A fable out of flame,
> Trees and spicy fronds and buds
> Forever game
> It is for such a man as I,
> Chosen not to choose;
> I live to love;
> A double muse. (Cook & Rubadiri, 1971, p. 173)

Taylor's poem presents a persona with love for two nations, which signifies two different cultures. The persona contrasts the two nations without a contempt for any one of them. One nation is hot, but the other is cold. One nation has rivers that flow smoothly, but the other is many violent water falls. These could signify that the former is a peaceful nation, but the other is laden with insurgency and rebellions. The crocodile is a symbol of pride and violence and is associated with this nation. One nation is wintry cold while the other is characterized by very hot summer. In the last stanza, the persona confesses that there is nothing he can do but accept his situation of double identity. He or she says, "I live to love / a double muse." The fever that is mentioned in the first stanza is a reference to ambivalence, which is a liking and disliking for something. For each of the two identities, there is something he dislikes and likes at the same time.

At the Junction

Andrew Nyongesa

> Scorching are the two roads,
> At the junction I stand.
> Heat from the two roads,
> My hair it withers;
> But am safe at the junction,
> Neither 't route one nor two;
> I am 't third.
> Two animals are vicious,
> At the middle I stand
> Pride from the two
> Compound my fears,
> But am safe at the junction;
> Neither bird nor mammal
> I am a bat.
> I love it when she flaps
> Flying long distances across seas;
> I hate it when she lays eggs
> Exposing her future to gangs of predators;
> Safe I sit at the middle,
> Neither bird nor mammal.
> I love it when she conceives within,
> Protecting her future from gangs of predators:
> I hate it when she treks long distances,
> Conquered by small ponds and lakes;
> Safe I sit at the junction,
> Neither bird nor mammal… (Mwanaka & Purificacao, 2018, p. 389).

The persona in this poem prefers being at the middle of two cultures. Whereas the two different cultures are very hostile towards each other, he stands at the third space where he can synthesize the attributes of the two cultures to survive in the cosmopolitan community. The persona refuses the hardline stance taken by the two communities in a binary opposition. He or she claims to be a bat, which is neither a bird nor a mammal. Ambivalence is evident when she shows a liking and disliking for birds and mammals at the same time. She loves the birds for flying but dislikes external fertilization in them; she loves internal fertilization in mammals, but hates their inability to fly. The poem is based on Homi Bhabha's concept of hybridity- the third space synthesizes attributes of essential groups thereby bringing to the end the politics of polarity in a cosmopolitan society.

4.4.2 Cultural Fixity in Bitek's Poetry

The song of Lawino and *The Song of Ocol* represent the views of the two essentialist groups: the Orient and the Occident locked in binary opposition. Ocol is an alienated academic speaking for the Occident and Lawino, the Orient, proud of the so called irrationality. Ocol accuses Lawino of irrationality, sensuality and all demerits characteristic of the orient as postulated by oriental scholars. In *The Song of Ocol*, he says:

> What is Africa to me?
> Blackness
> Deep, deep fathomless
> Darkness
>
> Africa,
> Idle giant
> Basking in the sun

Sleeping, snoring
Twitching in dreams

Diseased with chronic illness
Choking with black ignorance
Chained to the rock
Of poverty

Stuck in stagnant mud
Of superstitions
Frightened by the spirits
Of the bush, the stream
The rock
Scared of corpses. (Bitek, 1972, p. 207)

    The advent of colonialism invents a cosmopolitan society, the whites interacting with Africans for decades. Ocol opts for alienation as a strategy to cope with foreign values. He has rejected African traditions in favour of western values. Having taken western education to advanced levels, he knows the ins- and -outs of it thereby so proud of it. In his view, there is nothing good in African culture. In condescending voice, he dresses down African culture hence creating the duality invented by orientalism: Occident/Orient. In the above text, we see black/white, ignorant/knowledgeable, superstitious/rational, dualities proclaiming Western culture as far better than African culture.

    The occident particularly singles out superstition to degrade the Orient. Ocol says the black man hears eerie noises form the lake side and sees snakes in the whirlwind. By this he implies that western logic is far better than African superstition, which is akin to lunacy.

The African houses his gods,
Or he carries them
On his head
Or on his shoulder
As he roams the wilderness (Bitek, 1972, p. 207)

In the western perspective, the African has no home that is why his home is described as a 'wilderness'. He lives with wild game, 'following the spoor of the elephant'. The orientalist attribute of irrationality is further depicted in Ocol's image of the child. He declares that the African is a child. Obviously, children have immature reasoning with lots of emotions. He says,

Child
Lover of toys
Look at his toy weapons
His utensils
His hut
Toy garden
Toy chickens
Toy cattle. (Bitek, 1972, p. 207)

In the eyes of Ocol, the West views Africans as caricatures on the world stage owing to irrationality. It has rendered them incapable of inventing superior weapons, building comfortable homes and establishing reliable economic activities (toy chickens/ toy cattle). The orientalist attribute of weakness is depicted in Ocol description of Africans as timid, unadventurous and scared of the unbeaten track. He implies that the occident is courageous, adventurous and ready to venture in unknown fields. Ocol says:

> Unweaned
> Clinging to mother's milkless breasts
> Clinging to brother
> To uncle, to clan
> To tribe. (ibid)

In this text, he accuses Africans of excessive love for their culture, which is shocking because he has extreme love for western culture. Ocol, a fixed character accuses Africans of cultural fixity. The Africans are just responding to the West, fixity therefore begets fixity and feeds on itself.

Ocol distastes weaknesses so much that he regrets having been born black. His relationship with Lawino is tense and hostile. Lawino opts for cultural fixity to combat fixity; she wholly and unreservedly embraces African culture and denounces Western culture as professed by her husband, Ocol. She denounces western forms of grooming among women:

> Ocol is no longer in love with the old type
> He is in love with a modern girl
> The name of the beautiful one
> Is Clementine
> Brother when you see Clementine!
> The beautiful one aspires
> To look like a white woman
> Her lips are red hot
> Like glowing charcoal
> She resembles the wild cat
> That has dipped its mouth in blood
> Her mouth is like raw yaws
> It looks like an open ulcer

> Like the mouth of a field
> Tina dusts powder on her face
> And it looks so pale
> She resembles the wizard
> Getting ready for the midnight dance. (Bitek, 1972, p. 42)

Lawino shocks us by casting aspersions on what most Africans at independence view as aspects of advancement. She does not even use a tongue-in-cheek voice but uses satirical, almost a sarcastic voice. Clementina is a caricature of the westernized, modern woman to depict her hostility and contempt for Western culture on one hand and adoration for African ways on the other. We are shocked at the images she uses to compare Clementina: she resembles the wild cat/ that has dipped its mouth in blood. The wild cat is a greedy nocturnal predator renowned for night raids on poultry and stashed beef in the kitchen. Her mouth is like an ulcer, the lipstick; to her is not beauty but a sign of bloody danger. The powder makes her resemble a wizard, another nocturnal symbol of evil. Her diction depicts spite for Western culture. Lawino attacks all Western related forms of beauty, for instance, she says such women have counterfeit breasts:

> Oh, my clansmen
> How aged modern women
> Pretend to be you girls
> They mold tips of cotton nests
> So that they are sharp
> And with these they prick
> The chests of their men. (Bitek, 1972, p. 44)

She now turns the attack on dances of white people. She says she loves the dances of her people and does not want lo learn the games and dances from the West. This is typical of Cultural fixity. She gives the reasons why she hates these dances:

> You kiss her on the cheek
> As white people do
> You kiss her open sore lips
> As white people do
> You suck slimy saliva
> From each other's mouths
> As white people do (p. 53).

The diction in this text brings out her contempt for Western culture, for Lawino African culture is ideal. The kissing is described as an exchange of 'slimy saliva'. She praises African dances, that the youth dance during the day and the songs they sing have relevant themes like broken love, shortage of cattle and they dance when sober (50). But the Western dances are performed at night when dancers are drunk. They do not sing as they dance, they are as silent as wizards (52), with female partners, not their wives. Lawino sees western dances as immoral. She further depicts her unreserved love for her culture by lauding those aspects that are incompatible with the contemporary society:

> Butter from cows milk
> Or the fat from edible rats
> Is cooked with *likura*
> Or itika
> You smear it on your body
> And the aroma
> Lasts until next day. (p. 68)

As much as this was good body lotion in those days, it is more reasonable to use the foreign lotions today. Lawino scoffs at the good from the West for the sake of fighting the occident:

> I confess
> I do not deny
> I do not know
> How to cook like a white woman
> I cannot use the primus stove
> I do not know how to light it
>
> Electric fire kills people
> They say
> It is lightning
> They say
> The white man has trapped
> And caught the rain cock
> And imprisoned it (ibid).

We wonder what is wrong with learning to use the primus stove. What is wrong to learn to use the electric cooker? She has been deceived that it is lightning that kills. Bhabha observes that all cultures are hybrids and indeed no society progresses without borrowing from the Other. Sticking to past cultures as Lawino does results in 'fetishism of identities'. Lawino has shown unreasonable affection for her culture and rejects those western inventions geared towards betterment of her life, which is the fruit of embracing cultural fixity. There are other modern African poets that follow Okot's example by using cultural fixity to attack modernity and watern culture. Let us discuss one of them:

4:4.3 The Clash of Titans- Tradition Versus Modernity: A Critique of Ongogo Evelyne's *Dichol and Other Poems*

Ongogo E. (2017) is an anthology of poetry that depicts the clash of dominant African culture with infiltrating western culture. In spite of the fast spread of western culture via urbanization and formal education, Ongogo takes cue from postcolonial scholars like Frantz Fanon and Okot P' Bitek and Chinua Achebe to resist foreign influences. Fanon (1961) observes that African Literature should restore the dented dignity of a colonized people. In his chapter "On National culture" in *Wretched of the Earth*, Fanon asserts that colonialism destroys national culture and disrupts the cultural life of a conquered people: "cultural obliteration is enabled by negation of national reality, banishment of natives, their customs and systematically enslaving of men and women" (166- 199). In Fanon's perspective therefore, African literature should not only have nationalistic themes but be literature of combat– to fight for the existence of a nation. Ongogo's *Dichol and Other Poems* is in Fanon's view, literature of combat to fight for the existence of African ways of life.

The poems are set in rural areas and towns in modern Kenya to depict clash of African and western cultures. Western culture infiltrates Kenyan society via urbanization, mass media, formal education and tourism and those who adopt it challenge the traditions of African people. Ongogo uses characters from towns and cities or those in the rural areas but affected by westernization to depict cultural clash. Dichol, for instance is a woman in the rural areas, but has imbibed western libralism in matters appertaining sexuality. She goes against the African traditions by being a mistress to many men in the village. "Ondigo has a Wife" is set in a rural area with characters that have lived in urban areas. Whereas the persona appreciates

Anyango as a true African wife, some villagers with western influence view her as unexposed and worthless. The two contrasting settings set stage for clash of cultures that traverses the poetry from the beginning to the end.

The major characters in the poems are either fanatics of western culture or ardent believers in African traditions and braced for a duel with the other culture. The woman Dichol, in the first poem from which the title is derived is absolutely estranged from the ways of her people. The African moral code encourages young women to marry on time to curb promiscuity. With the advent of western values, young women today keep many boyfriends, which the persona attacks in the poem. Like Lawino and his co-wife, Clementine, the persona in "Dichol" attacks Dichol's lasciviousness. First, the persona attacks her vanity. Most African cultures (especially in western Kenya) despise vanity- the emphasis on physical beauty at the expense of character. The persona says:

> Dichol my beautiful sister, listen to me
> Yes, I know of your beauty
> Today, you have scrubbed your feet for hours
> With the black rugged pumice from the African riverbeds… (Ongogo, 2017, p. 10)

The persona's repetition of beauty in the first stanza is unrelenting attack on the modern woman's obsession with physical beauty at the expense of character attributes typical of responsible motherhood. Dichol spends a lot of time scrubbing her feet; as a consequence, she becomes lazy. In the proceeding stanza, the persona says, "You have rejected the oil of your age/ but smeared the alien sap" to suggest that Dichol applies cosmetics and other Western synthetic chemicals to conceal aging. The persona attacks her synthetic beauty by likening her to a leopard. Her attempt to look like white people flops and Dichol ends up with a speckled pattern of a leopard. The persona derides Dichol's sexual licentiousness, which she attributes to modern or western influence. The twigs *ochol* and *Sangia* know the number of Dichol's teeth. The image is probably a snide reference to Dichol's amorous nature; many male lovers kiss her and thereby know the number of her teeth. The bushes are personified as complainants against Dichol's bent on plucking them. The image possibly suggests the numerous time he is seduced by men in the village. The housewives are aware of the scent of Dichol's perhaps because she makes love with their husbands more often. The persona advises Dichol to go for her own perfume- husband- as prescribed by the morals of her people. Dichol is a product of new cultures in the community that do not cherish marriage and the persona views her as immoral and misfit of sorts.

In the poem "African Queen," Ongogo uses an anonymous conservative character to celebrate the beauty of the African woman. The poet romanticizes African beauty and culture. She suggests that African women ought not like Dichol yearn to resemble white women in looks. They already are beautiful icon(s) of creation (p.13). Their beauty is not just in looks but in diligence and wisdom. They are diligent because they are the "strength and backbone of Africa" and "unlazy lot of humanity". They are wise because even the cosmos "listens to your wisdom'. The poet suggests that African beauty, unlike the vanity of western culture, lies in looks and above all character attributes like diligence and wisdom.

The character Ondigo also depicts the clash of African and Western culture. In the poem "Ondigo has a wife" the persona who is an African traditionist is used to contrast the expectations of marriage in African and western or modern culture. In Western (modern) way of thinking, singleness is allowed in men. Celibacy is an option and men can forego marriage for career pursuits or religious reasons. Ondigo possibly inspired by one of the aforesaid reasons is single to a late age.

> They said you bored their young wives
> With your unending odes,
> That to them the word *shemeji*
> No longer made any sense but insult...
>
> They said your own mother prayed night and day
> To see smoke bellow from the left corner of your roof (p.22)

Ondigo bows to the pressure of his people and eventually gets married to a simple girl called Anyango. It is at this point that traditional African attitudes and modern (western) attitudes come in conflict. The persona defends Anyango against Western thinking. For the western way of thinking, a wife should have smooth feet, brown as the city girl, have formal education, know diverse soaps, and cook diverse dishes with a recipe. African culture on the contarary does not entertain strident demands on a wife appertaining physical appearance. The persona says, "even though they say Anyango's cracked feet are size four/ that her legs are the size of *oboroi* weed/ and her buttocks are flat as the indian *chapatti*/ ondigo you have a wife" (p.22-23). Moreover, the persona defends Ondigo that a wife need not have Western (formal) education:

> Even if they say
> Anyango did not see the front page of a book
> That she does not know the size of a pencil
> And the colour of a blackboard
> Ondigo, you have a wife! (p. 23)

In the African perspective, a wife need not know how to use a recipe to prepare exotic meals like a chef. As long as Anyango knows how to make porridge for all elders and her in-laws then she is a wife to be accepted by all. The persona adds more attributes of the African wife to deal western culture a blow: Anyango knows how to dig the farm (she can stay still sunset on the farm), she knows the roles of motherhood (Anyango can breastfed as she bends fetching vegetables; she can bear children (she bore the most lads in the village).

The character Ogilo in the poems "Ogilo Part I: This thing you call "Valentine" and Ogilo Part II: After Valentine," is alienated from the ways of his people. Ogilo is a diehard laity of Valentine day but the wife (who is African traditionist) reprimands him for showing her love on Valentine's Day only. On this day, Ogilo insists that she should not call him Ogilo Titus but Valentine or Valentino. And not just that, she should add "MY" owing to the nature of the day. The meals should be served on red and not white plate and the bed should not have blue pair of sheets but red. (p.30). But after Valentine's Day, Ogilo does not express any love at all. He almost sneezes when she calls him "My Valentine" (p.34). He spits when she complains about his tendency to love once in a year. When she asks to be loved, Ogilo replies that she should stop being an immature village adolescent. The persona suggests that modern (western) culture encourages people to love only once in a year unlike traditional times when anytime was Valentine.

Ongogo E. (2017) is about the clash of African tradition with Western ways that infiltrate society years after colonialism. The cultural conflict manifests through marriage, love, African tradition, widow inheritance, modernity and other themes through which the poet underscores the superiority of African culture over foreign influences. In the first poem, "Dichol" Ongogo portrays modernity (westernisation) as the root cause of moral decadence. Dichol's exposure to modernity makes her promiscuous and unable to settle down with a husband. Obala's embrace of western education makes him proud and flouts societal morals. Obala inherits widows without consulting elders because he feels he is too knowledgeable to. Since he had been a rich man possibly because of his high level of education, he does not heed advice from elders in the village. Persona says:

> Obala when society spoke
> You said they were young and knew nothing
> And that you were experiences enough
> You ate porridge in Atiga's house
> Even after seeing the size of the corpse
> Even when you saw the red lips
> You said all colours were equal
> And drank from her pot
> Where other men like you
> Only stared from far   (p. 46-47)

Obala's obsession with western culture inculcates in him stubbornness and insensitivity to morals that paves way for his destruction. In the poet's perspective, it is not African culture that makes people vulnerable to demerits of widow inheritance; it is the arrogance from western influence that makes people exposed to such perils. Ongogo suggests that traditionally, elders were involved in widow inheritance and a widow who had a dreadful disease from a husband would not be inherited. The inheritor had to be an in-law or related to the departed and elders had to assess the situation before sanctioning it. But Obala, the offshoot of modernity, flouts all this. The persona in the "inheritor" says:

> Obala you are not related to the late
> Yet you camp for a fortnight
> Consoling a widow many years below your age
> You did not even create space for your in-laws
> And mother to whisper words in her ears. (P. 40)

The clash also manifests itself via marriage, pitting modern marriage against traditional ones. In the poem "My husband", the persona is a modern wife influenced by western novelties. She reveals that her husband complains that she does not give him true love as she is alienated by media. She sends love messages, but the husband wants traditional love expression- person to person. The husband asks, "[w]hat are full stops! What are commas!" (p.56). The communication technology and studying have desensitized her; the smartphones, televisions, computers have drained her emotions and cannot connect with her husband. The husband complains that she "pours all the emotions intended for him on paper and screen," (56). She is probably a writer. The poet suggests that traditional African marriages were better than western skewed modern marriages because the spouses were untainted by modern devices like mobile phones and computers. The husband romanticizes the simplicity of traditional marriages where communication was person to person and brought more happiness in marriage.

Towards the end of the anthology, Ongogo openly elevates African tradition and demeans modernity (western influence). In the poem "The African woman," she romanticizes African culture and continent:

> A strong woman
> The beautiful one from the dark clay o'
> African richness

You creature of substance
With richness of love
With golden tears
Elevened on her cheeks (p. 81)

Unlike Okot P' Bitek who presents the African woman in the negative, Ongogo gives a positive view of the African woman because she signifies African culture. She suggests that in spite of the struggles Africans experience, their ways are not objectionable. The physical environment too is blessed with flowing rivers, green vegetation and others. The poet follows this with the poem, "I will not go to Town" in which she derides western influences:

I say I will not go to town
Where all spaces are co-owned
I will not go to a place where
Even the patio-
The opposite neighbor claims;
Where will I dry my corn?
I ask where? (P. 83)

Towns, which represent western culture, are portrayed as poverty stricken places where there is no space for daily chores like drying clothes, corn, sneezing and even breathing. They are overpopulated and people compete for essentials of life with dogs. The hygienic standards are low with heaps of rotting rubbish. At a deeper level, the poet uses the decadent imagery to suggest the moral decadence in western culture. The persona describes the women of the city as "fat city women" and men in the city as "hungry vultures" of the city. Gluttony is therefore a feature of western culture that manifests via urbanization. As the poem comes to a close, the persona opts for African culture:

> I will not divorce my language
> And speak those exotic city languages
> With rules and regulations
> I will talk the indigenous language
> That *nyopija*- my mama taught me   (p. 85)

The poet then proceeds to invite alienated Africans to African ways in "I Beckon you to the Village" (p. 86). The rural area, which is representative of traditional African culture, is surfeited with fresh fruit unlike urban areas where stale fruits are sold. The fruits are not defiled with the touch of many hands like those in towns and cities. The rural areas have fresh chicken unlike towns where people eat broilers conserved in fridges for months. This poem signifies the worth of African food in contrast with western diets that have made people vulnerable to illnesses such as cancer, heart diseases and infertility.

Ogongo employs a number of stylistic devices to express the cultural clash and superiority of African traditional ways to western culture. First is the free verse style as opposed to metric verse that is dominantly used in modern poetry. Free verse is prose masquerading as poetry because the poet defies the metric patterns in which there is regular distribution of stressed and unstressed syllables in stanzas. Such poets also use rhyme and alliteration to create rhythmic units. Instead, Ogongo chooses images form the local environment and extravagant repetition typical of African songs as a kind of defiance against western style of writing poetry. Let us analyse the following example:

To you Son of my in-laws
I warn you!
Do not say I did not warn you
When the parrot perches on your roof!
I have talked
When the kestrel still smiles on the cow's back!

If you only give me the kind of love
Where you clutch a pen between your teeth
Erasing words from a paper
To the umpteenth time to make things right   (p. 18)

It is evident from the above example that the poet uses prose, the common language of speech, in poetry. Verse is usually more compact than the above lines; however the images in the stanzas make them poetic. The images of the parrot and kestrel have a symbolic significance; they portend evil in the life of persona's husband. Pen and paper are derived from the persona's environment and represent modernity. Like P' Bitek, Ongogo rejects the western metric verse to imply that Africans too had poetry, which they expressed via repetition and imagery from the local environment. The poet also uses African words side by side with English to suggest that some meanings could be lost when these words are translated into English. Such words include *abuu* (traditional musical instrument) that is better understood by the native community: *Achego,* a type of sandy soil (that foreigners may not know) and *Akala-* traditional locally made shoes. The poet also employs burlesque, a type of satire that trivializes esteemed subjects and glorifies what is considered low. Ongogo trivializes western and urban ways of life, which are held in esteem in African societies. Urban ways are considered as symbols of exposure and knowledge; however, the poet trivializes them and elevates rural life and tradition. The style plays a pertinent role in expressing the poet's attitude towards the African and western cultures.

Ongogo (2017) is therefore an anthology about the clash of African and western cultures with rural and urban areas as the battlefields in the contemporary society. Unlike the colonial period when western culture directly made incursion on African values by colonialism and Christianity, westernization spreads via urbanization, the media, formal education and information and communication technology. In the contest of cultures, the poet takes a side to castigate western culture by creation of personas and characters that symbolize the cultures. Although the poet comes to a passionate defense of African culture, she partly portrays the culture as ancient, characterized by poverty, but has to be appreciated. True African women like Anyango stand out as unattractive, illiterate, and unexposed and only know how to cook porridge. While those that embrace western culture such as Dichol, though immoral, are pretty, assertive and exposed. Can African culture not borrow some elements from the West and still survive? Do we have to stick to the ignorance of cooking only porridge to be true Africans? Can men like Ogilo not marry more knowledgeable wives who still embrace Africa culture? Is a wife just but a woman who can only bear children? African culture can accommodate new ideas via a process referred to as hybridity and still remain relevant. The more Africans embrace new cultures, the better they can resist western culture from the point of information.

4.5 Postcolonialism and William Shakespeare

Many literary scholars have questioned Shakespeare's treatment of the race question in his dozen plays. Non white characters commit queer and foolish errors and suffer greatly behind the mask of fate. Shylock and the Prince of Morocco in the *Merchant of Venice* embody evil possibly because they belong to the marginal group in the society. This subsection employs the postcolonial theory to interrogate Shakespeare's treatment of race in *Othello*.

4.5.1 Othello, a Racist Play: A Postcolonial Critique

Othello like *Merchant of Venice* has raised the eye brows of many postcolonial critics about Shakespeare's treatment of the race question. His handling of so called oriental characters has been brought under the postcolonial microscope for detailed scrutiny. Both Othello and Shylock are of Eastern origin, the former is a moor from North Africa and Shylock is a Jew. Shakespeare's treatment of these characters was aimed at pleasing the racist Elizabethan audiences as influenced by Orientalist scholars.

Orientalism was a phenomenal work in postcolonial literary theory by the Palestinian US based scholar Edward Said. In his work he postulates that European orientalist scholar's divided the world into two essential groups: The West also called the Occident and the East, the Orient. They assigned these groups essential attributes, for example the East was described as irrational, lecherous, feminine, savage, inhuman and lying passively waiting to be conquered by the masculine West. Being lecherous, the Eastern men were a danger to the delicate white women. For Frantz Fanon, the white race had a certain fear for the Negro and Easterner because being biological without many intellectual pursuits; it is assumed he is sexually stronger than the white man whose libido reduces due to many intellectual goals. Fanon describes it as an unfounded fear because those white women who have made love with negro men never seen much difference. The racism in Fanon's view is motivated by the ID. Said expounded that the West was described as rational, humane, sexually stable, and masculine poised to conquer the East. He writes:

Europe is powerful and articulate. Asia is defeated and distant. It is Europe that articulates the orient, this articulation is a prerogative not of puppet master, but of a genuine creator whose life giving power represents the otherwise silent and dangerous space beyond familiar boundaries. The orient insinuates danger. Rationality is undermined by Eastern excesses. (57)

These orientalist ideas are depicted in Shakespearean plays to excite Elizabethan audiences of the time. Shylock, in *Merchant of Venice* is denied his rights just because he is a Jew. Why should Antonio condemn usury? What are the modern Bankers after? Is it not interest? Worse still, Shylock's daughter, Jessica is stolen by the Christian, Lorenzo and the court takes Shylock's wealth and gives it to the thief. Shylock is then forced to become a Christian against his will. It is this anti Semitism that led to the holocaust during the Second World War when Hitler fulfilling the wishes and archaic beliefs of his society, killed six million Jews.

4.5.2 *Othello*, the Orientalist Play

First is the orientalist belief that the East is irrational. Othello is given a choice between good as endowed in Desdemona and villainy as symbolized in Iago but his limited powers of judgment drive him towards Iago. The force of evil gradually asserts control over Othello's character and within three days he has become the barbaric villain, he ought to have been as a moor. Iago's cunning is exciting to the racist audiences since there is no way a black man can be as intelligent as a white man. And Shakespeare deliberately gives Iago high intelligence and Othello, foolishness. He judges everything by appearances and this is one aspect of idiocy: Iago says in a soliloquy:

"[t]he moor is of free and noble nature that thinks men honest that but seem to be so," (29). For example he trusts Iago so much and refers to him as, "honest Iago" just because he seems honest. He even entrusts him with his wife while at war in Cyprus. He has appointed his wife Emilia to be Desdemona's servant.

Because in the orientalist eyes the Moor is full of base natures, Othello is a man of strong passion. When he loves, he loves completely and when he is jealous, he hates absolutely. He is a man of extremes just as the orientalists observe, "[r]ationality is hampered by Eastern excesses." He tells Desdemona at Cyprus, "[w]hen I love you not, chaos is come again". He has sacrificed all his reason on the altar of passion. Love is his heaven without which he dies. He tells Desdemona, "I have gathered up my heart, where I must live or die to be discarded thence," (39). In the simplicity of his heart, Othello is like Child who says if father does not love him then he dies. When he solely depends on Iago to tell him his wife's infidelity, it is a child-like innocent wonder around him. Othello's decision to elope with a white girl is a symbol of lechery and irresponsible sex leveled against the orient- the East and Africa. And Iago sees nothing good in their relationship. When they kiss before him he tells Roderigo, "[l]echery, by this hand, an index and obscure prologue to the history of lust and foul thoughts," (40). It is manifestation of deep seated jealousy for the Easterner and unfounded phobia for his sexual powers.

Othello does not take time to find the actual facts. He keeps concealing Iago from Desdemona. Why can't he summon Iago before Desdemona and Cassio and ask him to explain his allegations? *The moor is impulsive as result of his weak intellectual capacity* is the orientalist belief and Shakespeare has to appease them.

The orientalist belief in the Moor's savagery is brought out in the way in which he becomes so angry as to faint. Just the imagination that Cassio is having sex with his wife infuriates him so much that he faints. Even his abilities as a soldier imply that the Moor can only fight but not think. When Iago tells him that Cassio talked in the dream and said, "sweet Desdemona," Othello says, "arise black vengeance from thy hollow cell!" (75). He then adds, "Blood! Blood! Blood!" Othello orders Iago to go and kill Cassio and proceeds to strangle Desdemona in the most savage manner. Desdemona's innocence is contrasted with Othello's barbarism as she calls him courteously up to the last moment: "will you come to bed, my lord?" (119). She represents the perfection of the white race as opposed to the retrogressive East.

The black race is associated witchcraft and black magic, in the play; they cannot even woo and win a beautiful woman unless they apply witchcraft. Brabantio accuses Othello of using black magic to win Desdemona:

> Oh thou foul thief, where have though stowed stowed my daughter?
> Damned as thou art, thou hast enchanted her
> For I'll refer me to all things of sense
> If she in chains of magic were not bound
> Whether a maid so tender, fair and happy
> So opposite to marriage that she shunned
> The wealthy curled darlings of our nation (15).

Othello gives a moving speech before the court and overthrows this argument. But Shakespeare with all oriental influences cannot believe that a black man can reason. He therefore introduces the magic handkerchief that Othello was given by his Egyptian grandmother and gave it to Desdemona. For the Elizabethan audiences, this was expected. The moor must have some charms to enchant his white lady. That strong cord of love between Othello and Desdemona is not genuine.

Othello is therefore a play influenced by Orientalist ideas that downgrade other races of the world. A reasonable man cannot behave like Othello, he is the fictitious belief of the racist whites about the East and Africa.

4.6 Postcolonial Critique of Genres of Oral Literature

Some African communities use riddles to subvert domination of African values by Western culture. Although riddles are word games performed by children for fun and environmental education, the underlying themes convey spiteful attitudes for western cultures. Look at the following riddles from Miruka O. (1994):

>Challenge: A European peeping through the window
>Response: Mucus (p. 29)
>Challenge: The white lady in the office
>Response: The Jigger (p.38).
>Challenge: The train running in the field
>Response: the centipede
>Challenge: the snake that exhales smoke.
>Response: The train (p.39)
>Challenge: On arrival at the station, I was shouted at.
>Response: A train. (p.39).
>Challenge: An Arab standing on one leg
>Response: The mushroom. (p.40).

The above riddles express the marginal groups spiteful attitude towards the dominant group. Africans demonstrate the spite they have towards western culture and indirectly reject its dominance by socializing the children to have contempt for the idea of white other foreign cultures. In the first riddle, the European is a metaphor for mucus. The tone is macabre and elicits a morbid response in the audience. Mucus is ghastly and many people would hate to talk about it in public. If the Europeans are associated with mucus then they are a by product of bodily functions just like feacal material and urine. In short, the children are being socialized indirectly to despise Europeans.

In the second riddle, the white lady is metaphor for a jigger. The jogger is hateful internal parasite common in mountainous areas of Africa. It develops from a flea and like lice, scorpions and other vermin, people must hate it. To this African community, therefore, the whites are parasites who work their way into the body of the African societies to destroy them. The children are being socialized to despise and avoid the vermin for their own good.

The third and fourth riddles compare the train to the snake and centipede. In most Kenyan societies, those who rear snakes are witches and witchcraft is the worst of evils. The centipede in Kenyan societies is feared for its poisonous sting and hence a negative image. The riddles warn children to be cautious with the novelties from the West. Some come with negative consequences. The smoke from machines (including the train) pollutes the clean air in the African environment. The noise from machines cause noise pollution and this is what the fifth riddle alludes to. The last riddle compares the Arab to a mushroom, a wild crop in traditional Africa. It grows near anthills- weak, untamed, estranged- by sheer luck and many a time trodden by livestock. The comparison therefore exhibits contempt for the Arab and his culture. Had he been compared with maize, millet, sorghum, wheat and other such food crops, it would have implied a liking for Arabic culture.

4.7 Conclusion

This chapter set off to examine postcolonial theory in diverse genres of literature. The author applied the theory on the novel, drama, poetry and oral literature. It is quite clear that postcolonial theory is an influential canon, particularly in African, diaspora literatures because of the cultural tensions created by slavery and colonialism. Its analysis of the domiant and marginal groups gives it a wide scope and it sometimes incorporates other canons like feminism since there a contest between the feminine gender as the marginal group and masculine gender as the dominant group.

REFERENCES
Abdolai, V. & Fatemeh P. (2014). Migration Literature; a Theoretical Perspective.*The Dawn Journal3.1*: P. 679-693.
Ashcroft B., Griffiths G., Tiffin H., (eds). (1995).*Postcolonial Studies Reader*. London: Routledge.
August, T. (2014). Out of Place: A Re-evaluation of the Poetry of Denis Brutus. (MA Thesis University of Western Cape).
Bailey, A. (1942). *Esoteric Psychology*. New York. Sun Centre.
Battersby, C. 1989. *Gender and Genius: Towards a feminist aesthetics*. Indiana University Press: Bloomington.
Bhabha H. (1988). Commitment to Theory.*New Formations,5*: P. 9-23.
Bhabha, H.(1994).*The Location of Culture*. London: Routledge.
Billing, M. (1989).*Arguing and Thinking: A Rhetorical Approach to Social Psychology*. Paris. Cambridge UP.
Bitek P.' O. (1972). *Song of Lawino and Song of Ocol*. Nairobi. E. A. E. P.
Chaytor, H. J. (1912). *The Troubadours*. Plymouth: The college.
Chinweizu et al. (1985). *Towards Decolonization of African Literature: African Fiction and Poetry and their Critics*. London: KPI.

Cinnirella, M. & Jaspal R. (2011). The Construction of Ethnic Identity: Insights from Identity Process Theory. *Ethnicities,12*: P. 503-530.

Cook, D. & Rubadiri, D. (1971). *Poems from East Africa.* Nairobi. EAEP.

Cooper, F. & Rogers B. (2000) .Beyond Identity: Theory and Society.*29:1*: P. 1-47.

Erikson E. (1968). *Identity, Youth and Crisis.* NewYork: W.W.Nortons Company.

Fanon, F. (1963).*The Wretched of the Earth.* New York: Grove Press, Inc.

Fanon, F. (2008). *Black Skin, White Masks.* Trans. Charles Lam Markmann. Oxon. Pluto Press.

Feder, L. (1980).Madnes*s in Literature.* Princeton, NJ: Princeton University Press.

Finkelstein, S. (1965).*Existentialism and Alienation in American Literature.* New York: International Publishers, 1965.

Fraser, R. (1976). *West African Poetry.* London, Cambridge University Press.

Fromm, E. (1956).*Sane Society.* London: Routledge and Kegan Paul.

Hall, S. (1990). Cultural Identity and Diaspora.In Rutherford, J. *Identity, Culture, Difference.* London: Lawrence and Wishart.

Hooks, B. (1981).*Ain't I A Woman: Black Women and Feminism.* Boston: South End Press

Imbuga, F. (1976).*Betrayal in the City.* Nairobi: E.A.E.P.

K.L. Godwin (1964). *Undertanding African Poetry.* Nairobi. H E P.

Kristeva J. (2001).*Melanie Klein.* Trans. by Gubermann, Ross. New York: Columbia University Press.

Laing, D. 1990 [1965].*The Divided Self: An existential study in sanity and madness.* London: Penguin Books.

Lau, E. H. (2008). The Migrant Experience, Identity Politics and Representations in Postcolonial London: Contemporary British Novels in Zadie Smith, Hanif Kureish and Monica Ali. MA Thesis University of Hong Kong.
Marrietta, M.(1984). Women's work, family and Reproduction among Caribbean Slaves. *Working Paper 76*. Texas Tech University, 1-10.
Leonard, L (1993). *Meeting the Madwoman: An Inner Challenge for the Feminine Spirit*. New York: Bantam Books.
Linfors, B et al (1972) eds, Palavar: *Interviews with Five African Writers in Texas*. Auxin: University of Texas.
Lupack, B. T. (1995). *Insanity as Redemption in Contemporary American Fiction*. Gainesville: University Press of Florida.
Miruka O. (1994). Encounter with Oral Literature. EAEP.
Morrisson, T (1987). *Beloved*. New York: Penguin Books USA Inc.
McClosky, H. & John, S. (1965). Psychological Dimensions of Anatomy:*American Sociological Review, 30*.
Nair, S. (1995). Melancholic Women: The Intellectual hysteric(s) in Nervous Conditions. *Research in African Literatures*, 26, 130 – 139.
Ngugi W. T. (1986). *Decolonizing the Mind*. Nairobi. H E P.
Nyongesa, A. (2017). At the Junction. In Mwanaka & Purificacao (Eds). *Best "New" African Poets 2017 Anthology*. Chitugwiza. Mwanaka Media and Publishing.
Okigbo, C. (1971). *Labyriths with Path of Thunder*. New York. Africana Publishing Corporation.
Ongogo E. (2017). *Dichol and Other Poems*. Nairobi. Royallite Publishers.
Papanek, P. (1994). Strangers and double self–consciousness: feminism and black studies. *Identity Politics and Women: Cultural Reassertions and Feminisms in International Perspective*, ed. Valentine M. Moghadam. San Francisco: Westview Press.

Pearce, A. (1990). *The Heinmann Book of African Poetry*. Ibadan. Heinmann Educational Press.
Pollard, V. (1994).*Homestretch*.San Juan. Longman Trinidad Ltd.
Portes A.& Rubiin R.(2005). Introduction: The Second Generation and Children of Immigrants Longitudinal Study: *Ethnic and Racial Studies, 28*: P. 983-999.
Reid, G. (2002). *A Re-examination of Tragedy and Madness in Eight Selected Plays from the Greeks to the 20th Century*. Lewiston: Mellen.
Rhys, J. (1997). *Wide SargassoSea*. Hermondsworth.
Ruganda, J. (1972). *The Burdens*. Nairobi: Oxford University Press.
Said, E. (1977). *Orientalism*. London: Penguin.
Saleem, A. (2014). Theme of Alienation in Modern Literature.*European Journal of English and Literature Studies,2*: P. 67-76.
Shakespeare W. (1968). *Othello*. London. Penguine Group.
Szasz, T. S.. (1971). *The Manufacture of Madness*. London: Routledge & Kegan Paul.
Sulyman, A. (2014). Theories of Identity Formation among Immigrants: Examples of People with an Iraqi Kurdish Background in Sweden. Linkoping University.
Ulli B.& Gerald M. (1963) Eds. *Penguin Book of Modern African Poetry*. London. Penguin Group.
Van, J. (2001).Interview with Dennis Brutus.*Alternation 8*: P. 168-215.
Wright, Richard. (1940). *Native Son*. London: Penguin Books.
Young, R. J.C (2003). *Postcolonialism: A very Short Introduction*. New York: Oxford UP.
Zubida. H., Lavi L., Harper A. R, Nakash O. & Shoshan A. (2014). Home and Away: Hybrid Perspective on Identity Formation in 1.5 and Second Generation Adolescent Immigrants in Israel. *Journal of Culture, Politics and Innovation, 1*: P. 2-4.

CHAPTER FIVE:

PSYCHOANALYTIC THEORY

5:1 Introduction

Psychoanalysis is derived from Freudian revolutionary psychology in which he developed the notion of the unconscious and others like displacement, fixation, condensation and manifest latent dream content. While expounding on Freudian concept of psychoanalysis, Tyson L. (2006) notes that human beings are driven by desires, fears, needs and conflicts of which they are unaware,' (p.12). Psychological criticism approaches a work of literature as the revelation of its author's mind. Tyson adds that literary works are linked to their author's mental and emotional characteristics (p. 34). Critics therefore explain how a literary work reflects the writer's consciousness and mental world and use what they know of the author's life to explain features of the work. Freud (1900) observes that there is a tight relationship between the creative action and the artist and the neuroses and the role of the unconscious in the artistic creation must be determined. In other words, there is a close relationship between the artist and dreaming and for that reason, the artist is sort of mentally ill.

Freud notes that the unconscious harbours forbidden wishes, desires- often sexual- that are in conflict society's moral standards. The individual represses these unconscious fantasies, which become displaced in dreams and other forms of fantansy. While elaborating on unconscious, Freud invented *psychic apparatus*. In short, psychoanalytic tenets are as follows:

Freud invented what he termed as psychic apparatus, which he defined as mental structures that direct human behavior. He talked about the ID, the part of the mind that contains the wicked desires, that is sex and destructive instincts. They occupy approximately ninety percent of the mind. He defined the EGO as the part of the mind that balances the ID and SUPER EGO. All reasonable acts of man emanate from the ego. He then defined the SUPER EGO as part of the mind that craves perfection as demanded by society.

Secondly, Freud identified dreams as an essential element of the psyche. For Freud, the unconscious thoughts of the ID force their way to the consciousness through dreams. The third tenet is phallocentric symbolism. Freud asserted that since the highest proportion of the unconscious is filled with primordial instincts like sex, man unconsciously makes objects that look like sex organs to express the repressed desires, for example pestle and mortar, spoon and bowl. Moreover, Freud expounded on psychological concepts such as fixation, defined as an obsessive interest of feeling about someone or something. Finally is displacement, which is unconscious replacement of something by a mere illusion.

5:2 Psychoanalysis and the Novel

The novel stands out as one of the creations of the mind by which the writer's neuroses manifest. The inspiration that guides the novelist to write down the story is to Freud a dream world that brings his unconscious to the fore. The forbidden wishes stand out clearly given the length of the novel. Its length is unlimited hence enabling the writer to bring out many psychological concepts like self defense mechanisms, psychic apparatus and phallocentric symbols.

5:2.1 The Unconscious and Patriarchy: A Psychoanalytic Study of Nawal El Saadawi's *God Dies by the Nile*

"He could see her firm rounded buttocks pressing up against the long *gabaleya* from behind," writes Saadawi of the mayor in her novel, *God Dies by the Nile* (p. 18). The sentence astounds the reader and lets him or her question the extent of rot among male characters in Nawal El Saadawi's society. This and dozen other texts in Saadawi (1985a), *God Dies by the Nile* suggest that there lies more behind the male psyche than the class struggle as many scholars claim. Creative writers, according to Freud, write from a dream world. The so called inspiration, for Freud is the unconscious world that brings out the primordial instincts of the human mind, namely, death and sex instincts. Saadawi (1985a), *God Dies by the Nile* depicts Freudian principles in an amazing manner. Koseli Y. (2013) analyses the correlation between the heroine's psychological traumas with the author's biography. He notes that Sadawi (1994), *Memoirs of a Woman Doctor*, begins with "the return of a female doctor to her childhood by focusing on the psychological trauma that she had experienced as a result of sexual discrimination" (p. 211). Koseli then compares the heroine's experiences with the life of Nawal El Saadawi who observed hardships and inequalities faced by rural women at Kafr Tahla as a young medical doctor. Koseli Y. (2013) concludes, in league with psychoanalytic principles, that a work of art reveals the creative writer's deepest spiritual happenings, personal concerns, fears, repressed aspirations and pains that he or she cannot overcome. The writer therefore 'displaces these repressed desires through writing' (Eagleton, 1990, p. 199). Besides attempting to unearth the writer's personal neuroses and unmet desires and wishes, psychoanalysis attempts to analyse character motivations in works of art. Many

Literary writers have written to reveal the role of the unconscious on human behaviour but few can rival Nawal El Saadawi. The author employs her background training in psychiatry to apply concepts of psychoanalysis to motivations of male characters. This chapter employs Freudian concepts of psychoanalysis to analyze motives of characters, and personas and investigate the relationship between their ID and patriarchy in Saadawi's *God Dies by the Nile*.

5:2.2 Synopsis of *God Dies by the Nile*

Set in sleepy hamlet, Kafr El Teen, *God Dies by the Nile* is the story of the struggle poor peasants and female characters against an unscrupulous, tyrannical Mayor. The Mayor is a shrewd politician who has infiltrated the people's religion to curve for himself a sort of personality cult of which consequence is abuse of peasant women. As a 'god' he directs sheikh Hamzawi, Haj Ismail and sycophantic, male, villagers to arrange his 'dates' with female candidates for abuse. Given his economic and political position, he goes about his life as a god-sovereign and omnipotent. No one can question his authority, violating and flouting maxims of decency. He is above all the villagers and sometimes tells them, "[t]o me you are all nothing!" (p. 15). Taking advantage of his libidinous natures, he ogles at girls and defiles them. Other male characters follow in his footsteps some forcing girls to marry them, beating women into submission and applying crude forms of circumcision to control their sexuality. The women have neither choice nor power, and those men who marry the girls the Mayor has defiled, like Elwau are murdered. Nonetheless, the female character, Zakeya, has had psychological problems resulting from the Mayor's tyranny and plucks up courage to kill him. Zakeya is embittered by the Mayor's conscription of her only son, Galal into the army, Mayor's arrest and detaining of her brother, Kafrawi, the

Mayor's murder of Elwau, her niece's husband and frustration of her niece, Zainab.

The principal characters of this study are the Mayor. He is the main antagonist in the novel and is used to portray the evils of patriarchy, which is justified by religion. His lust for girls depicts him as man of roaring ID. Zakeya is the prime mover and protagonist of the novel. She is the major mouthpiece of Saadawi and harbours bitterness against the patriarchal system embodied in the Mayor. She has a psychological problem as a result of the oppression that stems from the patriarchal system. Sheikh Metwali is yet another character who in spite of his piety commits unspeakable abominations. He exhumes corpses after burial to have sex with thereby depicting the hollowness of patriarchal piety. Kafrawi is another important character in this study. He is Zakeya's brother whose two daughters, Zainab and Neffissa become victims of the Mayor's lust just because he has designs on them and does not want them to marry Zakeya's son, Galal. Sheikh Hamzawi is the cleric in Kafr El Teen who maintains a cordial relationship with the Mayor but finally falls out with him because he has a beautiful wife, Fatheya. The Mayor's henchmen assault him for adopting what they consider an outcast child that presumably invites Allah's wrath by drought. Elwau is yet another character in this study; he is the Kafrawi's son-in-law who flees with Neffisa. The mayor is so infuriated that he sends his henchmen to kill Elwau

5:2.3 Psychoanalytic Critique of Saadawi's *God Dies by the Nile*

Saadawi (1985) *God Dies by the Nile* abides by Freudian psychoanalytic principles. It is possible that elements of the unconscious motivate her characters to commit unspeakable acts. Let us begin with Zakeya, the peasant woman who kills the Mayor in the story. The story begins when she is digging her farm: "[n]ow the hoe could be heard thudding out over the neighbouring field with a steady sound and it cut deep into the ground," (p. 3). The hoe and the farm are phallocentric symbols; the hoe represents the penis and the farm, her female reproductive system. The cutting into the earth is unconscious reference to the sex act. The aggressive cutting is a displacement, shift of energies to digging due to her waning libido. The writer says, "[h]er body no longer stood upright," (p. 3). It could no longer respond to sexual excitement. Unconsciously, Zakeya manifests both the Eros and death instincts in this instance, which in Freudian terms they can either work separately or concurrently. The narrator says:

> The blows of her hoe seemed to echo with an anger buried deep down as she lifted it high up in the air and swing it down with all her might into the soil. The blows resounded with their regular sound like the muffled strokes of the clock. (Saadawi, 1985a, p. 3)

In Freudian terms, Zakeya's digging is sex instinct and the anger is the destructive instinct, which destroys relationships. The Eros enables her to form relationships with Kafrawi, her brother, Galal, her son and Zeinab, her niece. The attraction Zakeya has towards her son and husband is the same, "[s]he could see her son, Galal sleeping beside her. She tried to put her arm around him; he seemed to move out of reach. A hand caught hold of her. She looked around to find her husband fast asleep" (p. 88). Zakeya's dreams and visions exhibit her unconscious. In one dream, she sees a high iron gate coming towards her as if to crush her, and a buffalo also comes as if to walk over her but her mother comes to save her (p. 87). Other nights she dreams standing on a hill, her body falls from high into the river but she swims and reaches the river bank. Then she finds herself at the irongate. Then she is lying on her mat with her husband Abdel

Moneim and her son on the other. The husband hits her pregnant belly and proceeds to have sex with her (p. 88). In Freud's view, sleep is a moment of uproar and chaos when unconscious thoughts of the ID try to force their way into the conscious. They result from conflict and bring up memories the dreamer has forgotten. The dream reveals Zakeya's turbulent relationship with her husband. Whenever she gave birth to a daughter, her husband would beat her. "Every time a son of hers died, he would strike out at her blindly," (p. 89). The instance of the Iron Gate having legs and threatening to trample on her signifies the injustices the Mayor has meted out on her brother, Kafrawi and other members of her extended family. It also foreshadows her conflict with the Mayor later in the novel. The irongate is a phallocentric symbol of the Mayor's penis. Zakeya sees the Mayor's libido as the cause of her suffering for he arrested her son, Galal for planning to marry Zeinab.

The Mayor of Kafr El Teen is another character that exhibits Freudian psychic apparatus. He is a man with a roaring ID, which he does not conceal. His elder brother is more successful than he and so displaces it by obsession with sex. As a young boy, his mother said to him, "[y]our brother is better than you are," (p. 14). True to her word, the brother is an influential politician while the Mayor is just a village leader. The writer says, "[t]he moment he had seen his brother's picture in the newspaper, a feeling of inadequacy and depression had come over him… as a child, he would run to the bathroom and vomit all the food in the stomach," (p. 14). He is psychosomatic as a consequence of jealousy, a destructive instinct arising from this sibling rivalry. He tells Haj Ismail, "[c]ompared to me, you people are just nobodies," (p. 15). These words are meant for his brother but he cannot find him to tell him. Even his laughter is just escapism from the inner turmoil he suffers as a result of his brother's success in the family. Furthermore, the Mayor smiles unusually when a beautiful girl is mentioned. He tells Haj Ismail, "[t]he youngest is always tasty," (p. 12). Sex instincts blossom when he looks at Zeinab. Narrator says, "[h]e could see her firm rounded buttocks pressing up against the long *gabaleya* from behind," (p. 18). Sheikh Zahran says that she has a strange taste where women are concerned. 'Once he sets his eyes on a woman, he must have her; come what may', (p. 70). Nonetheless, his Eros works hand in hand with destructive instincts. Her love making with Zeinab is described as follows:

> His hands were now sliding on her thighs to her belly as he tried to lift her garment higher. But it was wet and stuck to her flesh. He pulled on it so hard that it split with rending sound. And he tore the remaining fold from around her body. (Saadawi, p. 64)

The tearing of Zeinab's clothes is a violent act that points to his destructive instinct, even as he desires to have sex with her. The two instincts again manifest when he kills Elwau after he flees with Neffisa, a girl with whom he had made love. He is even jealous when Hamzawi marries Fatheya, a beautiful girl. He schemes and arrests Galal for marrying Zeinab, a girl he had sex with. He has Hamzawi ruffled up for adopting a child claiming that he has brought evil on the land by adopting a bastard, Fatheya is killed while trying to save the baby: "Fatheya's clothes were torn away and her body shone white, and naked like that of a terrible mermaid in moonlit night," (p. 145). The Eros instinct assists him to form relationships with his wife who he lusts after right in the house, he "ogles at her bare thigh beneath the skirt" (p. 51). He also forms relationships with Haj Ismail and Sheikh Hazran, who brings him the girls he lusts after.

There are several phallocentric symbols associated with the Mayor: at the beginning the narrator says:

> He loved Cairo. The lamps shining on the dark surface of the tarmac roads. The coloured lights of the river side casinos reflected in the flowing waters of the Nile. The night clubs thronged with eating and drinking as they sat around the tables, the women dancing, their bodies moving, their perfume and soft laughter going through him. (p. 12)

The casino and night club represent sex, which he is obsessed with. The women dancing and bodies moving is the act of sex to him. The lamps represent his penis and the flowing Nile waters, the female reproductive system. The image of the iron gate associated with him is his penis and roaring appetite for sex; the Mayor is fixated at the genitals.

Apart from the Mayor, sheikh Metwali is the most eccentric character in *God Dies by the Nile,* a man whose ID has trampled on the super ego in spite of his virtuous title. Like the Mayor, he is fixated at the genitals because he roams at night to exhume corpses to screw. He would exhume corpses:

> And if it was that of a female, he would crawl over it until his face was near the chin. If it was male, he turned it over on its face then crawled over it until the lower part of its belly pressed down on the buttocks from behind. (p. 74)

These sexual perversions are manifestation of the wicked instincts in his unconscious mind. His death instincts manifest in the way he seeks his bed among the dead. The writer says, "[h]e lived among the dead year by year," (p. 73). Apart from having sex with corpses, the Eros enables him to form relationship with women. Women who met him would ask for a blessing. He would stretch out his hand and squeeze any part of their body he wished as saliva flowed down his beard (72). The body language in this instance is very phallocentric. Stretching out the hand represents his penile erection. The salivating mouth means that he imagines the vaginal orgasm. There is also displacement because he cannot have sex with these women by virtue of his status as sheikh, he opts to bless them but in reality, he fondles them to derive sexual pleasure.

Sheikh Hamzawi is the cleric in Kafr El Teen Mosque. He is a close ally to the Mayor but he arranges for his murder because Hamzawi has a beautiful wife, Fatheya. Although the Mayor claims that Hamzawi is punished for picking an abandoned baby, which is bad omen, the truth is that Fatheya is beautiful and the Mayor wants her to slake his lust for sex. Sheikh Hamzawi stands out as a man with roaring ID. He is quite aggressive towards the opposite sex in spite of his impotence. He admires Fatheya and compels her to marry him against her will. Surprisingly, he does not have the potence to break Fatheya's virginity. The traditionist, Om Saber, is invited to break her virginity. The writer observes, "Fatheya felt the burning pain left by the woman's finger as it probed up between her thighs looking for blood," (41). The destructive instinct stands out when he advises Haj Ismail and Masoud to beat the bride, Fatheya, to force her into marrying him (p. 40). He also loses temper and hits the adopted child. Eros is also manifested in ability to forge relationships with those around him for example Haj Ismail, the Mayor, and Fatheya. He teaches her how to pray and recite the Koran. The phallocentric symbols associated with Sheikh Hamzawi are his dimmed eyesight that signifies infertility or inability to sire children (p. 45). He is in possession of a stick that he uses to tap on the ground as he walks around. It signifies his penis. There is displacement in his life as he has substituted his infertility with fanatic love for religion.

Kafrawi is Zakeya's son and father to Neffisa and Zeinab, beautiful girls who the mayor has designs on. Nefissa rejects the

Mayor's advances and marries Elwau who is murdered by the Mayor out of jealousy. The Mayor demands for Zainab to serve him in his house but Kafrawi objects because he needs her for daily chores. Kafrawi is arrested, which infuriates Zakeya bitterly.

Kafrawi is portrayed as a man of roaring Id, for example, the act of suckling the buffalo is phallocentric in itself. It resembles the act of sex and he goes further to have sex with the buffalo (p. 61). There are tendencies when the sex and death instincts work hand in hand. The narrator says, '[t]he penis slid up into the inner warmth and was lost in great stillness, like an eternity, like death," (p. 61). The eros enables Kafrawi to establish relationships with his daughter, Neffissa. They play around in a phallocentric manner, "[h]er small hand would play with his whiskers. He opened his mouth, closed his lips over her smooth fingers.' This signifies sex instinct, '[b]ut one day he bit her fingers with his teeth," [p. 60]. Here is the sex instinct turning into destructive instinct.

Kafrawi's dreams depict the death and sex instincts. In his dream he sees the dead body of his mother lying on the ground, which turns into the body of Elwau, the dead son-in-law. The sex instinct in this dream comes in form of Freud's Electra complex, where children are sexually attracted to their mothers and change to learn their sex roles due to the fear for their fathers. The appearance of Elwau's corpse is manifestation of the destructive instinct. The main phallocentric symbol associated with Sheikh Hamzawi is the female buffalo- Aziza. According to Sigmund Freud, Sexual perversion is as a result of fixation during early stages of development. Kafrawi is fixated on sex hence the bestiality in his personality.

Finally, Elwau is the young man who loves Neffisa, Kafrawi's daughter and flees away with her to the Mayor's annoyance. He is later pursued and killed by the Mayor's henchmen. On one hand, Elwau portrays sex instincts when he recalls how he was sodomised by his cousin, Yousef, "Yousef caught him in an iron grip holding him by the back of his neck, threw him to the ground face downwards and wrenched his *galabeya* up his buttocks. He felt the powerful, heavy body press down on him…" (p. 66). Eros instinct is apparent when he is able to form strong relationship with Neffisa. She rejects the Mayor, '[r]efuses to go the irongate,' and flees with Elwau. His destructive instincts are evident when he walks around the village without greeting anybody. The narrator says, "[h]e was always silent, never spoke to anyone nor turned his head to look at a shop…" (p. 53).

5:2.4 Psychoanalytic Critique of Patriarchy in *God Dies by the Nile*

Nawal El Saadawi is a strident critic of male dominance and violation of women and girls world over. In her biographical novel, *Woman at Point Zero*, the heroine Firdaus grows up like any other girls with hopes and aspirations. Her father dies and leaves her in the hands of the uncle who sells her to sheikh Mahmoud. The rich sheikh abuses and makes her pay for every cent he spends on her. The suffering drives her out of marriage and Firdaus cohabits with Bayaumi who also starts abusing her. Firdaus meets the harlot, Sherifa Dine who introduces her to prostitution as a mode of resistance against male dominance. In the story, 'The Picture,' in *She has no Place in Paradise*, Saadawi attacks sexual immorality in men. The man of the house, Nirji's father uses Nabawiya, the house help as a sex butt. In her essay "Hidden face of Eve," Saadawi decries this practice, which is embraced in Egyptian families where fathers and their sons use housemaids to meet their sexual urges. The same sexual violations recur in *God Dies by the Nile* where the Mayor hires Kafrawi's daughters, Neffissa and Zainab, and rapes them to gratify his sexual desires (p. 69). Many other unspeakable sexual abominations are committed by male characters in

Saadawi's *God Dies by the Nile:* male characters falling in love and having sex with animals, having sex with fellow males and worse still, there are male characters such as sheikh Metwali who exhume corpses to have sex with. Iyabode (2014) observes that Saadawi portrays men in a very terrible light hence bringing the didactic value of literature in question (p. 123). One of her characters, Sherifa Dine in *Woman at Point Zero* says, "[m]en are dogs running around under various names." Although Iyabode (2014) interrogates Saadawi's propositions, literature to a great extent is a mirror of society. As psychoanalytic critics observe, the writer's work has a close connection with his or her life experiences. Saadawi has observed these sexual abominations and calls for change among men in her society.

Shihada, I. (2007) argues that class is the major factor that precipitates patriarchy and violation of women in *God Dies by the Nile*. He notes that men take advantage of their influential positions to oppress and dominate women. On the contrary, scholar Mitchell, J. (1974) singles out Freudian psychic apparatus as one of the factors that contribute to patriarchy and violation of women world over. Mitchell observes, "[t]he Marxist revolutionary must link arms with Freudian Psychologist in order to effect women's full and final liberation," (p. 412). She suggests that any change in the status of women should be accompanied with the defeat of capitalism as well as change of men's psyche towards women. As much as wealth and influence contributes to patriarchy, Freudian psychic apparatus such as the Id broadly contributes to male domination and violation of women. Mitchell (1974) suggests that men have a stronger Id than women hence more vulnerable to sexual and violent indignities, which is quite evident in Saadawi's *God Dies by the Nile*. Brownmiller (1975) points out that "[t]he secret of patriarchy lies in rape, which is the act of forcing a woman to have sex against her consent," (p. 209).

Saadawi's characters apparently demonstrate the presence of a stronger ID in men than women which leads to violation of not just feminine gender but fellow men, animals and the dead. The Mayor's sexual lust is, according to Freud, engraved on his mind rather than the result of his high social class. As the story begins, Saadawi (1985) contrasts between the Mayor and his elder brother who is in a higher social class than he:

> The Mayor, loved city life of Cairo, the lamps shining on the tarmac roads... night clubs... the women dancing... their bodies moving...their soft laughter going through him. At the time he was a college student. But unlike his elder brother, he hated lectures and lecture rooms... above all, he hated his elder brother discoursing about politics and political groupings. (P. 12)

The Mayor who does not work hard in college and is comparatively a failure in life exhibits higher levels of primitive instincts of sex (ID). The night clubs symbolize sex and in his thoughts are dominated by erotica: women dancing, their bodies moving and women's soft laughter appealing to him. His jealousy for his elder brother represents the destructive instincts characteristic of the ID. When he looks at the mirror, he sees his successful brother saying, "I succeed in everything I undertake, but you have been a failure all the time," (P. 14). The Mayor's low sense of achievement is displaced by contempt at men of his class and violation of women of his class. He tells Haj Ismail, "[c]ompared to me, you people are just nobodies," (15). Apparently, low class men in Saadawi's novel exhibit higher levels of sex instincts and violation of women. While the Mayor is chatting with fellow villagers like Haj Ismail, Zeinab happens to pass by. Haj Ismail makes a sexy remark about Zeinab, "[t]he younger is always most tasty," (p. 18). The remark so excites the

Mayor and he looks at Zeinab, "[h]is eyes followed the tall lithe figure of Zeinab as she walked along...he could see her firm, rounded buttocks pressing up against the long *gabaleya* from behind," (18). Whereas members of the high society such as the Mayor's brother are interested in political power and other important things that affect the country, the poor men are only interested in primordial instincts of sex and destruction. Men with more education tend to have more knowledge about the rules that guide society- Freud's super ego- thereby commit few or no sex scandals. Shihada's proposition that class is the root cause is only partly correct otherwise how would we explain the tendency of men of low social cadres exhibiting high degrees of patriarchy and violation of women?

Sheikh Hamzawi belongs to the low social cadre but portrays extreme patriarchy and violence towards women. He tells Fatheya's father that women should not make any decisions in the house including the choice for husband. "Beat her, my brother... do you know that girls and women are only convinced if they receive a good beating?" (40). The same primordial instincts are depicted in Abdel Momoneim, Zakeya's husband. The narrator says that every time, Zakeya's husband "struck out at her blindly with anything he could lay hands on" (89). He could also beat her whenever she gave birth to a daughter. It is not the high cadre in society that drives men to exhibit patriarchy rather it is the poverty and ignorance of the low society, which underscores Freudian savage instincts of sex and destruction. Zakeya has undergone so much pain that it projects through dreams. She experiences funny visions. In one of her dreams, she sees Om Saber leaning over her, push one thigh away, pull out the razorblade and proceed to cut her neck, (p. 88). Her bitter attitude towards female circumcision having denied her sexual pleasure is firmly locked in the unconscious, which expresses itself through dreams.

Although Om Saber is a woman, she exhibits tremendous levels of patriarchy. The female circumcision she carries out on thousands of women is the very pinnacle of male dominance. Whenever she appears in a woman's house, she is only interested in destroying their private parts to weaken them in the presence of men. This owes to her obsession with the ID because the cutting is the destructive instinct and the private part symbolizes her sex instinct. A classical example is when Om Saber mechanically breaks Fatheya's virginity to give Sheikh Hamzawi power over her. The narrator says, "Fatheya felt the burning pain left by the woman's finger as it probed up between her thighs looking for blood," (41).

5:2.5 *God Dies by the Nile* and Saadawi's Mind

In her biography, Saadawi (1999) entitled *A Daughter of Isis;* Nawal El Saadawi was born in 1931 at Kafr Tahia in Egypt. She was the second born child in a family of nine. She was circumcised at the age of six, an experience that she did not like at all. Her father insisted that his daughters had to learn and Saadawi pursued her studies to university level, graduating with bachelors in medicine and furthered in psychiatry. In her work experiences as a young doctor, Saadawi observed the hardships and inequalities faced by rural women and her heart went out for them. At one point, she attempted to protect her female patients from domestic violence and she was summoned back to Cairo. Saadawi's marriage life is a complicated one: she married her first husband, Ahmed Elmi for two years only. She later married Sherif Hetata and divorced him after forty three years.

Let us now focus on the correlation between Saadawi's life and her novel, *God Dies by the Nile*. We realize that there is similarity between the setting of the novel and her place of birth. Both are small villages, the novel is set in a small village called Kafr El Teen, and the author was born at Kafr Tahia. The village experiences in the novel reflect her real experiences in her native village.

The fact that she was circumcised at the age of six years is an important detail that affects her writing of *God Dies by the Nile*. Saadawi does not conceal her hatred for female genital mutilation. Om Saber is a caricature that clearly depicts her hate for the rite. Om Saber attracts love and hate simultaneously. Saadawi actually satirizes traditional surgeons who have joined hands with men to institute patriarchy through female circumcision. Of Om Saber, she writes:

> Going from house to house, helping women in labour, circumcising the girls, piercing holes in their ears. At weddings, she would paint the feet of girls and women with red henna...at night tear the virgin's haymen with her finger... she was busy solving the problems of girls and women: carrying out abortions with a stalk of *mouloukheya*, throttling the newborn baby if necessary (Saadawi, 1985a, p. 92).

Om Saber's contribution, although introduced in the positive is summarily negative in the sense that she breaks the girls' virginity to conceal the men's impotence, she circumcises girls to make them sexually powerless before men and worst of all carries out abortion, which is inconsistent to the teachings of the religion professed by the majority in Kafr El Teen. In her biography, Saadawi (1999), she reveals her spite for female circumcision when she says, "[t]his wound in my body has not only not recovered since my childhood but also left behind a deep mark in my soul," (p. 74).

Saadawi's experiences with female patients as a young doctor are depicted in her female characters. We are told in her biography that she sympathized with female victims of domestic violence; in the same vein, she sympathises with Zakeya, Fatheya and other female characters who suffer physical abuse by husbands in *God Dies by the Nile*. Of Zakeya, she writes, "[e]very time a son died her husband Abdel Moneim struck out at her blindly with anything her hands lay on," (Saadawi, 1985, p. 89). The reader is shocked at the cruelty of men in this society; Monein beats a wife with fresh wounds of delivery. Zakeya's suffering has caused her so much mental anguish that it projects through dreams: "[h]er husband kicked her belly...he began tearing her *galabeya* down the front till her body was exposed" (p. 88). Saadawi empathizes with her heroine, Zakeya so intensely that the reader feels the full weight of her burden, most of which is caused by male dominance. The domestic violence by her husband, death of her babies, arrest and detention of her brother, Kafrawi, oppression of her nieces (Neffissa and Zeinab) cause immeasurable pain that compel her to kill the mayor.

The writer's marriage life portrays her as a person who has had her issues with men and is resentful towards them. Saadawi's first marriage lasted for two years and she broke the second after forty three years in it. Her frustration in the marriage institution seems to have developed in her bitter feelings towards men. In *God Dies by the Nile*, male characters are portrayed as depraved and immoral people who practice rape, adultery, fornication, bestiality and homosexuality. They are also depicted as wife barterers, hypocrites and impotent. The worst characters, with a shameful love and sex life are Kafrawi and Shekh Metwali. Kafrawi falls in love with a female buffalo, Aziza and establishes a soul connection and communication with it. The writer says, "Kafrawi started to speak to the buffalo"... (p. 60). Then one day while suckling her, he loves it so much that he has sex with it:

> He felt something fill up, become swollen and erect... he watched it get out... slowly it crept over the soft udder, breathing in the smell of female, lapping up the familiar wetness, slid up into the

inner warmth and was lost in great stillness, like an eternity, like death. (p. 61)

More shocking is Sheikh Metwali who exhumes corpses at night and "if it was that of a female, he would crawl over it until his face was neat the chin. But if the body was male, he turned it over on its face," (p. 74). That a man can only live all his life having sex with corpses is an absurd overstatement by the writer that is aimed at attacking sexual abuse of women in the society.

Freud described creative writers as people who nurse inaccessible dreams and wishes and escape it by writing. What could Saadawi's wishes and dreams be? What are her emotional characteristics?

First, Saadawi wishes to kill all men who oppress women but lacks that ability to do because of existing laws. The wish is depicted in his character, Zakeya who is so angry with the mayor for presiding over a patriarchal system that violates women and girls. At the end of the story, she picks the hoe and strikes the Mayor dead.

Secondly, she dreams of a Marxist society without the religious ideology that encourages the oppression of women. Zakeya is the author herself leading women to overthrow religion and capitalism to free women and girls from oppression. In the character of Zakeya, the author suggests that religion does not solve women's problems; it magnifies them by compelling them to submit to the oppression of men. At Al Sayeda Mosque, Zainab is instructed to go to the mayor and will find a solution to her problem (p. 115). Zakeya's problem is said to be caused by rebellion to the patriarchal system. At personality level, Saadawi is depicted as bitter about men because they violate the rights of girls and women. She is also quite jealous men and feels they enjoy sex and power over women. Her description of sex scenes, even rape, comes out in a quite captivating way to signify her admiration for manhood. She describes the way the mayor bathes Zainab, dries her in a soft towel smelling jasmine and carries her to bed to have sex (p. 126). Her jealousy for manhood is also apparent when she looks at girls in a lustful male ogles. Of the mayor, she writes, "[h]e could see her firm, rounded buttocks pressing up against the long *gabaleya* from behind" (p. 18). In Saadawi (1985b), *Müzekkirât Tabîbe*, she confirms that while growing up, she was ashamed of her femininity. This shows that she has always wanted to be a man and hence envies men. She writes:

> I got out of the bed, posed against the mirror and looked at the two small hills growing on my chest. I wish I could die just at that moment. I was totally unable to recognize this body which dragged me from shame to shame everyday and increased my weakness. What new changes waited for me in my body. (p. 4)

The jealousy compels her to exaggerate priorities of men, for instance, she seems to suggest that men will always enjoy sex even if they have it with corpses (Sheikh Metwali) and animals (Kafrawi). In real life, men enjoy sex with those women they love rather than corpses and animals.

5:2.6 Conclusion

In conclusion, *God Dies by the Nile* is a feminist novel in league with Freudian principles of psychology. It is also apparent that patriarchy is not as a result of men's access to wealth and status but rather inherent in the primordial instincts of the mind. For if access to the means of livelihood were the major predisposing factor then there would be no violation of women in the low cadres of society. Saadawi's characters in the low stratum of society exhibit high degrees of rape, domestic violence, bestiality, sodomy and murder. The Mayor, who appears to be of higher class is in fact a failure as opposed to his elder brother, a politician based in Cairo. The elder brother, though a man has not a single sex scandal to his name. Patriarchy, if related to class, is not commensurate to class but is a consequence of inherent instincts in the ID that break the banks if left unrefined by education and weak ego.

5.3 Psychoanalysis and Poetry

Poetry is yet another area through which creative writers exhibit Freud's psychic apparatus. Writing from a dream world, creative writers manifest their unconscious through poetry to extremities. As mentioned earlier, dream and vision is one form through which Christopher Okigbo and Ezra Pound used to write their poetry. In this section, we corroborate the thesis that psychoanalysis traverses all genres of literature without going back to Okigbo. Read the following poem:

Rhythm of the Pestle
Richard Ntiru

Listen, listen-
Listen to the palpable rhythm
of periodic pestle,
plunging in the proud perfection
into the cardial cavity
of maternal mortar
like the panting heart
of the virgin bride

at each succeeding stroke
the grain darts, glad to be scattered
by the hard glint
of the pestle's passion

During the aerial suspension
of the pendent pestle
the twice asked, twice disappointed girl
thinks of the suitor that didn't come… (Amateshe, 1989, P. 92)

The main feature of psychoanalysis in this poem is phallocentric symbolism. The notion that sex dominates the unconscious processes in humankind and leads us to make objects that resemble sex organs clearly stands out in this poem. The mortar and the pestle unconsciously represents the female and male sex organs and the crushing of nuts that is the surface meaning of the poem is lovemaking, which is in fact the deeper meaning of this poem. The mortar is described as "maternal" mortar to suggest womanhood. As the poem unfolds we realize that the poet is talking about consummation of a marriage after wedding. Phallocentric symbols assist in effective depiction of the subject. Let us psychoanalyse another poem:

A leopard Lives in the Muu Tree
Jonathan Kariara

A leopard lives in the Muu Tree
Watching my home
My lambs are born speckled
My wives tie their skirts tight
And turn away-

Fearing mottled offspring.
They bathe when the moon is high
Soft and fecund
Splash cold mountain stream water on their nipples
Drop their skin skirts and call obscenities.
I am besieged
I shall have to cut down the muu tree
I'm besieged
I walk about stiff
Stroking my loins
A leopard lives outside my homestead
Watching my women
I have called him elder, the one from the same womb
He peers at me with slit eyes
His head held high
My sword has rusted in the scabbard
My wives purse their lips
When owls call for mating
I'm besieged
They fetch cold mountain water
They crush the sugar cane
But refuse to touch my beer horn.
My fences are broken
My medicine bags torn
The hair on my loins is singed
The upright post at the gate has fallen
My women are frisky
The leopard arches over my homestead
Eats my lambs
Resuscitating himself. (Cook & Rubadiri, 1971, p.65)

The persona in this poem is a very frustrated and disgruntled man. The audience wonders why he is not happy even as he laments about a leopard that lives adjacent to his home. In the wild, the leopard is a symbol of violence, which to Freud is a destructive instinct in the unconscious. The leopard eats the persona's lambs. Eating to Freud is a sex symbol because the hand takes the food into the mouth imitating the act of sex. The persona "walks about stiff" and "stroking the loins" as a proof of his miserable existence. For Freud, man can only be miserable if he misses the greatest reward: sex. From this point, we analyse the poem for any deprivation of sex. The persona says that the women "fetch mountain water" but refuse to "touch his beer horn". The horn is a sex symbol and in this context represents his manhood. Why do the wives refuse to touch his manhood? The persona says his "medicine bags are torn [...] and the upright post at the gate has fallen". The image of the upright post is phallocentric; it signifies the penis and the falling suggests that he has erectile dysfunction. The torn "medicine bags" suggest a low sperm count, which has rendered the persona infertile. This confirms Fraud's assertion that the greatest reward for man is love making. The persona is hopeless because he cannot have normal sex relationships with women and sire children. The leopard is therefore an elder brother who sires children for him. Persona says, "I have called him elder/ the one from the same womb." He comes in the evening when the wives are bathing outside in a makeshift bathroom to mate with them. This is possibly the family's arrangement to enable the persona have children to ward off shame. Jonathan Kariara effectively employs psychoanalytic principles to convey a sensitive subject to the audience.

The Town Beauty
Magemeso Namungalu

There she lay in a pool of blood,
Speared and maimed
Mute and lifeless
Base and worthless.

There she lay, the butchered woman,
The butchered woman, daughter of a chief,
Daughter of a chief, the town beauty,
Silenced by the rage of a spear.

She lay in a pool of blood, nude as she was born,
Fierce as if hours ago not lovely to touch
Already beginning to steam like fresh dung:
No one knew she was daughter of a chief.

She lay mid a group of frightened women-
Women who were mad with grief
Men that were there fumed with fury
That a beauty should enter the ground so young.

There she lay, silenced forever,
With her beauty crossed,
Her eyes for ever shut to the world;
Soon the ground was to swallow her. (Cook & Rubadiri, 1971, P. 107)

The main psychoanalytic feature of this poem is phallocentric symbolism. A beautiful maiden has been speared to death and the villagers are angrily mourning. There is a mournful mood because the girl has died prematurely in spite of her exceptional beauty. The persona suggests that the death was cruel by mention of the words, "the butchered woman." The butchering for Freud is a destructive or death instinct that dominates the unconscious. He adds that sometimes death and sex instincts work simultaneously such that very cruel people are also sex maniacs and will rape women and defile children. The spear to Freud is a sex symbol that represents the penis. We therefore should examine the poem and see whether there is any act of sex. Several proceeding words and lines suggest that the girl was not killed by a spear. On the first stanza, the poet uses the word "base" to describe the corpse. 'Something base' is something unclean or defiled. Why is the girl's body "defiled" if it was killed by the ordinary spear? In the third stanza, the girl is "nude as she was born." We ask ourselves why a murderer should undress the girl to kill her by a spear? The second line brings us to the deeper meaning of the poem, "fierce as if hours ago not lovely to touch." The line suggests that some men had touched or fondled her body hours ago. The women are "frightened" and the men "fumed with fury". The women are frightened because they are possible victims of rape and men are angry because their sources of sex are being contaminated. It dawns on us that the girl in the poem was raped and there the spear is just a metaphor- a phallocentric symbol.

How do you live?
Andrew Nyongesa

> How do you live in that cave,
> A lifetime of abyss?
> How do you perceive beauty?
> Lonely man behind shrouds.
> Just your Maker knows why,
> You live behind the shrouds.

How do you live in silent world,
Life akin to the grave?
How do you live without music,
Songs and dances that excite?
How do you live without sweet words
To those you love and care for?
Just your Maker knows why
You live in total silence.

How do you live without family,
A lonely life like that of a lunatic?
Why do you miss pleasures and comforts,
Fine things that measure success?
Why do you do all chores by self,
Just your Maker knows why
You live without family! (Nyongesa, 2013, P. 45)

The persona in the first stanza pities those who are visually challenged. Whereas we credit him for being merciful, it is surprising to note that he pities the visually handicapped because they cannot see beautiful women and to start enjoying the great reward of sex as Freud asserts. For the persona, those who fail to see beauty- sexy figures of ladies around cannot be happy. In the second stanza, the persona sympathises with those with hearing problems because they cannot hear love songs (songs and dances that excite). For Freud, singing and dancing is sex and those who like just displace their sex feelings. The other reason he pities the deaf is that they cannot speak romantic or sexy words to those they love. The pity revolves around the subject's inability to enjoy sex to qualify Freud's assertion that the human's mind is dominated by sex instincts, which come in a writer's moment of inspiration- dream or vision.

In the last stanza, the persona pities celibates, bachelors and spinsters who have no family. This stanza echoes Freud's assertion of the precedency of lovemaking in the life of humankind. The persona refers to sex as "fine things that measure success?" the society considers one as very successful if he or she has family. Family does not just signify reliable and legitimate source of sex but one has done it successfully to fertilize conception. A soccer player who makes more scores is revered so is a potent man.

5.4 Psychoanalysis and Oral Literature

Freudian psychoanalytic principles are evident in African folklore both short forms and prose forms. The psychic apparatus, phallocentric symbols and other psychological concepts such as condensation and defense mechanisms manifest clearly in African folklore. Let us begin with prose forms: songs and oral narratives:

> There lived a beautiful girl called Sela. The story of her beauty visited every home in the world. But Sela loved pleasure. She loved song and dance; she adored *ilitungu*. *She* would surrender her soul to any man who knew how to play it.
>
> One day, Mwambu, her elder brother, went for a stroll. When he reached the river, he saw Sela picking *enderema*; he got elated. He knew that in the evening he would have a meal he had missed for a very long time. At supper time, Mwambu bounced in, braced to enjoy *enderema* only to find the usual cowpeas.
>
> "Where is the *enderema* I saw you picking?" thundered Mwambu
>
> "I didn't go to the river today," replied Sela.
>
> "You're a liar!" roared Mwambu and slapped her.

Sela wept and returned to the kitchen. She did not blame her brother; he rarely beat her. She resolved to visit the river to unearth the root of her troubles.

She rose at sun rise and headed for the river. She found a dark fat girl, exactly like her picking enderema. Sela was very veeery shocked. She had met her own ghost.

Reliving her fate the previous night, she decided to greet the girl.

"Mulembe yaya."

"Mulembe swa."

"Me, they call me Sela," she introduced herself.

"I am also Sela," the stranger, said.

They embraced, both surprised.

Sela told the stranger the experience she had had the previous evening. Sela Two agreed that he had seen a man pass by with a gaze that suggested that he knew her. She proceeded to welcome her to their home but warned her that she was the only human being in a family of monsters. When they reached home, Sela Two said that the man eaters had gone hunting and would return with song and dance.

"When they come," instructed Sela Two, "don't come out however sweet their songs are."

"I won't," affirmed Sela One.

"I'll dig a pit in the compound and hide you there," suggested.

Sela Two, "and don't be tempted by the moving songs please."

"I won't sister," persisted Sela One.

After the evening meal, Sela, sister to ogres, dug a deep pit behind the store and hid Sela there. She covered the mouth with banana leaves. The ogres arrived, lively. The home was thrown astir with merry songs and dances accompanied by crotchet beats of the drums. They thumped their feet, shook their shoulders and clapped their hands; the result was a moving *kamabeka* dance. Their voices mixed well to produce a harmonious song. They sniffed their noses around and caught a visitor's scent in the home. They sang a song to express it:

Sela mekeni muya kaunya muno
Sela mukeni muya kaunya muno
Sela mukeni muya kaunya muno
Sela mukeni muya kaunya muno

Sela we've smelt a visitor's scent
Sela we've smelt a visitor's scent
Sela we've smelt a visitor's scent
Sela we've smelt a visitor's scent

Sela was astonished at their sensitivity and sang another moving song to dissuade them that there was no visitor on the compound. She named them one by one:

Okanakhundia papa okanakhundia
Okanakhundia Wamukobe okanakhundia
Okanakhundia Wamalabe okanakhundia
Okanakhundia mukeni kamayena

Want to swallow me dad want to swallow me
Want to swallow me Wamukobe want to swallow me
Want to swallow me Wamukobe want to swallow me
Want to swallow brothers, where do I find a visitor?

Sela's voice was sweet but it did not convince the monsters. They enlivened their dance and thumped their feet with an amazing passion. What vigour! They plucked their matungus skillfully; SelaOne inside the pit died of pleasure. She swayed her body to the slightest change of rhythm. She forgot all her fears. She forgot warnings. Those sweet voices that soothed her passion would not kill her. It was Sela Two's sheer jealousy to deny her a moment of happiness. She danced, danced and danced. She climbed up the pit, threw away the banana leaves and joined the frisky dance. The ogres rejoiced to see the food and danced more vigorously.

Sela we've smelt the visitor's scent
Sela we've smelt the visitor's scent
What we said was true
Sela we smelt the visitor's scent.

The ogres then began licking Sela; the foolish girl thought they were attracted to her. They stopped licking her and tore her skin. They stopped singing and scrambled over the parts of her body. She whimpered and called Sela One to no avail. Nobody could save her from the hands of these man eaters. They ate all her flesh, deserted the bones in front of the store and went to sleep.

The following morning, Sela Two woke up and seeing her friend's bones wept at her foolishness. How could she risk her life for a dance? She went to the bush and plucked a branch from the tree, *lufufu*. She arranged the bones in position and lashed them. Sela came back to life. Sela Two warned her never to be lured by song. She vowed to obey.

Whenever the monsters came and sung their song, Sela would sing her song and they would apologize:

Ndomakhandio luweni ndomakhandio
Ndomakhandio Kichwa ndomakhandio

I'm just joking Luweni I,m just joking.
I,m just joking Kichwa I,m just joking

Sela One would not come out of the pit. Days went on. One day SelaOne said,

"Come with me so that you live with human beings. It's hard to stay with ogres,"

"True," affirmed Simbi and proceeded, " Sela Two agreed on condition that nobody called her ogre.

They reached home and Mwambu was very elated to welcome them. He found it very hard to distinguish between them but her sister had a gap in the teeth that Sela Two lacked. After few days, he married Sela Two vowing never to call her ogre. One day after drinking busaa, Mwambu stood up and shouted, "These are the disadvantages of being born among ogres!"

Sela picked a rope, ran to the banana farm and hanged herself."(Nyongesa, 2018, p35-39)

The story begins with reference to Sela One's beauty, which to Freud either singles out her vulnerability to sex predators or liking for it. The next sentence asserts that Sela One "loved pleasure". From Freudian psychic apparatus, Sela loves sex and this sets stage for domination of the sex instincts in this story. The song and dance that Sela One delights in is to Freud, sex, which she unconsciously displays through them. The act of cooking in the kitchen, which Sela One has to do for family is a phallocentric symbol. In African societies, food signifies sex. If a husband refuses the wife's food, it signifies his hatred for the wife particularly in bed. Girls are socialized to know how to cook and serve food to signify serving the husband in bed. The eating that Mwambu wants do is phallocentric. Why is it just men who are associated with eating? The ogres who go hunting to eat, judging by the names, in this story are men. The sweet songs the ogres sing are lovesongs which men use to cheat girls and since it is night,

Sela One is foolish to join them. When she appears at the arena, she is the only girl dancing with men. The licking signifies the undressing and eating is an act of rape. Sela One is raped by Sela Two's male siblings. Realise they do not imagine eating Sela Two which means they cannot have sex with Sela Two because it would be tantamount to incest. The use of *lufufu* for resurrection of Sela One possibly suggests that Sela One was wounded but did not die. Sela Two nurses her to recovery using herbal medicine and warns her to keep off from men at night. She adheres to his advice and finally takes Sela Two to her home. Mwambu with penchant for "eating" spots her very fast. His earlier tendency to beat the sister suggests intense sex instinct that culminates into patriarchal dominance. He falls in love very fast and the marriage to Sela Two signifies sex instinct in the story. His false promises that he would never call her an ogre which he does signify the destructive instinct. Sela Two's decision to commit suicide is manifestation of the death instinct.

5:5 Split Personality, the Extension of Psychoanalysis

Modern psychology has had a lot of impact on literature and it would be absurd to discuss psychoanalytic principles without a mention of split personality and other theories that fragment the self. Proponents of the fragmented selves like Roanald Laing look upto Sigmund Freud as the hero that inspired them to study the human mind. Like psychoanalysis, split personality is an influencial theory in modern literature. A study of Japanese literature gives a unique flavour in the way these writers explore the psychology of characters. From Kenzaburo Oe, Ibuse Masuji through to Haruki Murakami, there is tendency of Japanese authors to introspectively explore the psychology of their characters. This subsection uses psychological criticism to explore the concept of split personality in Oe's *Silent Cry*.

Kenzabure Oe explores psychological disturbances of his characters to reveal mental distress that bedevils them. Some of these anomalies result into withdrawal, masturbation, violent behavior and suicide.

5:5.1 Introduction

Psychological criticism reflects the effect of modern psychology on literature. Authors and critics apply the principles of modern psychology, for instance, Psychoanalysis, self defense mechanisms, split personality and many others. Modern psychologists define split personality as a coping mechanism that stems from severe trauma during early childhood, for example repetitive physical, sexual and emotional abuse. The symptoms include two or more distinct identities that control the individual, the distinct identities have their own age, sex, posture, gestures, way of talking and the patient switches to the one he wants; depression, mood swings, sleep disorders, appeals to self punishment, night terrors, sleep walking, anxiety, phobias, hallucinations- seeing things that are not real and delusions- believing things that are not real.

Split personality may result into depersonalization- a sense of being detached from one's body or out of body experiences; derealization- a feeling that the world is not real. Amnesia, which is failure to recall significant personal information and self punishment- the feeling that one must punish himself because he is guilty of wrong doing. He or she does not want to enjoy a moment of peace.

5:5.2 Split Personality in Japanese Literature

As observed earlier on, Japanese authors tend to explore the mental problems of characters in their works. In *Black Rain*, Ibuse Masuji explores the psychological impact of the atomic bomb on the populace of Hiroshima. The characters are haunted by the destructive effects of the bomb and resort to the writing of private journals to manage these heightened stress levels. Overwhelmed by the painful realities of the bombing of Hiroshima, Iwatake writes in his private journal, "[t]he bodies were laid out in a heap at one end of the sports ground, with nightfall, the moans became more anguished. Those with brain fever leapt out of the window and started walking through paddy fields," (p. 248). As Shigematsu walked through the street in Hiroshima he says the people were all bleeding from the head, from the face, from the hands and those who were naked bled from the chest, from the back, from the thighs and "[a]ny place from which it was possible to bleed,"(p. 44). The journals in *Black Rain* are symbols of the psychological problems that Japanese characters face in attempt to reconcile with the effect of the atomic bomb in the novel.

Haruki Murakami in his story, *The Mirror* presents a character who suffers quite a lot after school. He later lands a job as a janitor in a school. One night as he is making his usual rounds, he undergoes depersonalization. He suddenly sees his own goes in an imaginary mirror. He says:

> After a couple of puffs, I certainly noticed something odd. The reflection in the mirror was not me. It looked exactly like me on the outside, but it definitely was not me. No, that is not it. It was me of course but another me. Another me that never should have been. I do not know how to put it. It is hard to explain what it felt like (Olembo& Emilia, 2010, p. 68)

The narrator is a victim of split personality as he undergoes an out of body experience thereby seeing his own ghost. The painful past of unemployment has planted a psychological anomaly in his life.

Oe's *Silent Cry* explores this theme in detail. The title *Silent Cry* represents the inner psychological confusion the characters experience as they attempt to cope with past traumas of life. The suicide motif in the novel yet another piece of evidence. Most of his characters have a deep seated void that they so much fear to confront hence plunge in split personality, a predicament which heightens their plights to death.

The first example of these characters is Takashi, the narrator's brother. Takashi is Mitsuburo's younger brother who leaves Japan for the United States in search for greener pastures. His charisma and charm gives him the outer image of success and happiness; nonetheless, he sustained an emotional wound that has eaten him all his life. As a result, he has developed a passion for violence to fabricate a punishment for his sins. In United States he leads a strike to oppose the US president visit to Japan since he sanctioned the atomic bombing, and the innocent Japanese students ignorant of his psychological ailment follow him to the vortex of danger. Scores are injured by security officers, Takashi rejoices because he has got punishment for his past errors. The guilt drives him to a whore and after sex, he says that what he wanted from her is far deeper than sex (p. 212).

Takashi has a split personality since there is a part of him that he hates and would rather do away with. These are the split identities that clash with each other within hence endangering his life. He tells Mitsu, "[t]he stronger the hope got, the more urgently I felt the need to wipe out that terrible side of myself… the more serious the split came," (213). His agitation and desire for strikes, even when he comes back to destroy the Korean's supermarket in the village, is far from selfless desire to fight for the weak. It is craving for self punishment, and the villagers follow him blindly. And he confesses, "[t]o go on accepting myself as I am. To justify myself as a man of violence," (p. 211).

Split personality began in Takashi's life after his incestuous sexual affair with his sister. The sister conceived and her uncle compelled her to abort and sterilized her. She had hardly recovered when she asked Takashi to have sex with her. Takashi refused and she rushed to the toilet and committed suicide (p. 238). Henceforth, he held himself responsible for his sister's death. After confessing to Mitsu, he declares a lynch execution for himself. Mitsu tells him that he has been looking for self punishment for the wrongs he has done:

> You are hopping to punish yourself for the incest and death of an innocent person that you brought about...I am hopping that if that fantasy becomes a reality, the two sides of your personality would come together again in death (p. 240).

Therefore split personality drives Taka to invent problems to get punishment. In Mitsu's view, he allowed himself to go on living without being punished, if he had got punished, he would have got healed. Therefore all claims that he had raped a girl in the valley and killed her are lies to incite the village against himself (p. 222). His decision to take Mitsu's wife and have sex with her is yet another way of courting his brother to kill him; however, Mitsu's low spirits cannot permit him to do that. Above all, he is intelligent enough to know that Takashi is a psychic wretch

Finally, Mitsu's friend possibly has a split personality. Mitsu says that he suffered severe psychological trauma such that he could not reconcile with his inner turmoil. He punishes himself by suicide, committed in a queer manner. He paints his head crimson, places a cucumber in the anus and hangs himself (P. 18). Before this, he had cut short his studies in Columbia due to mental problems. At the smiling training center, they are given tranquilizers and trained to smile. The nurse takes advantage of this to assault them. Mitsu's friend stops using them and beats up the nurse; he is expelled from the hospital. Towards the end of the story, Mitsu tells us that he could not share something inside him that had made him kill himself (p. 269). He implies that the guilt had split his identity.

Split identity is therefore one of the silent cries in Oe's *Silent Cry*. The writer explores the harrowing effects of this psychological condition in the society.

REFERENCES

Brownmiller, S. (1975). *Against our will: Men, Women and Rape*. New York: Simon and Schuster.

Eagleton, T. (1990).*Edebtyat Kurami*. Instabul: Ayrinti Yayinev.

Freud, S. (1900). *The Interpretation of Dreams*. London: Horgand.

Ibuse M. (1969).*Black Rain*. New York. Kodansha International.

Iyabode, D. (2014). Nawal El Saadawi and the Woman Question. *Journal of English Language and Literature, 2*, 121-124.

Kariara, Jonathan. A Leopard Lives in the Muu Tree. In Cook D. & Rubadiri D. (1971).*Poems from East Africa*.(P. 64-65). Nairobi. EAEP

Khaleeli, H. (2015). Nawal El Saadawi: Egypt's Radical Feminist. *The Guardian*.

Koseli, Y. (2013). Psychoanalytic Approach to Elsaadawi's Memoirs of a Woman's Doctor. *The Journal of International Social Research, 6*: 171-211.

Mitchell, J. (1974). *Psychoanalysis and Feminism*. New York. Vintage.

Murakami, Haruki. The Mirror.In Olembo W. & Ilieva E. (2010).*When the Sun Goes Down and Other Stories*. (p. 64-70). Nairobi: Longhorn Publishers.

Namungalu, Magemeso. The Town Beauty. In Cook,D& Rubadiri, D. (1971). Poems from East Africa. (P. 107). Nairobi. EAEP.

Ntiru, Richard. Rhythm of the Pestle.In Amateshe, A., D. (1989).*An Introduction to East African Poetry*: (p. 92-93). Nairobi. EAEP.
Nyongesa A. (2013). *Dissecting Poetry*. Nairobi. Splendour Publication Agencies.
Nyongesa, A. (2018). *The Water Cycle*. Chitugwiza.Mwanaka Media and Publishing.
Saadawi E., N. (1980). *The Hidden Face of Eve: Women in the Arab World*. London: Zed books.
Saadawi, E., N. (1983). *Woman at Point Zero*. London: Zed Books.

-(1985a). *God Dies by the Nile*.London: Zed Books.

- (1985b) *Müzekkirât Tabîbe*. *Cairo*: *Dâru'l-Me'ârif.*

-(1987). *She has no Place in Paradise*. London: Methuen.

-(1994). *Memoirs of a Woman's Doctor*. London: Methuen.

-(1999). *A Daughter of Isis*. London: Zed Books.

Shihada, I. (2007). The Patriarchal Class System in Nawal El Saadawi's God Dies by the Nile. *Nebula. 5:* 162-182.
Tyson, L. (2006). *Critical Theory*.New York: Routledge.

CHAPTER SIX:

STYLISTICS- THE MAGIC WAND

6:1 introduction

Writers address similar issues in society whether from the field of sociology, philosophy, politics, history or literature. Some address the corruption that bedevils the society while others address social issues like gender disparity and female circumcision. In this chapter, the author employs the stylistics theory to demonstrate that it is style that distinguishes a literary work from other philosophical, political, historical and sociological works. All writers the world over write about philosophy, politics, history, family, economy, education, and other similar issues, but what distinguishes a literary work from the rest is style. It is the novelist's techniques that the writer uses to shape, explore, define and evaluate his subject. Khattak Mohamed et al observe that the farthest ranges of the writer's art, the depth of his or her experience and the height of his or her spiritual insight are expressed only through an examination of his art (p. 98). Therefore the writer's intention, attitude towards the subject and central themes in the work can only be reached by examination of his or her style. This chapter employs the stylistics literary theory to explore the role of style in transforming an ordinary historical, philosophical, sociological and political work into a work of art.

6:2 Definition of Style and Stylistics

Kane and Peter define style as a pattern of linguistic features distinguishing one piece of writing from another. To them style therefore includes the writer's way of thinking about his or her subject and their characteristic way of presenting it for a particular reader and purpose (34). It is therefore apparent that it is style that distinguishes a work of art from a philosophical work. Furthermore, style distinguishes one novelist from another because literary writers have unique ways of presenting their subjects to their audiences. G.H. Windowson (Cited from Khattak Mohammed et al) observes that stylistics has an advantage of illustrating how particular linguistic forms function to convey specific messages. It can therefore compare types of texts (literary and non literary) in order to ascertain how they fulfill different functions (98). Windowson clarifies that style entails the choice of linguistic forms by the literary and non literary writer to convey messages. Without style both literary and non literary writers cannot convey themes. The literary writer will choose a unique way of presenting his or her message since literature is an art, and art constitutes beauty. Paul Simpson notes that the preferred object of study in stylistics is literature because it is institutionally sanctioned art or noncanonical form of writing (3). Literature is therefore unconventional form of writing and because style makes it so, it becomes a major concern for stylistics. Some critics have objected the stylistic evaluation of language of a text with claims that it destroys the text's aesthetic value. Mohamed Khattak et al reject this objection by observing that the acquisition of how something is manufactured does not make us lose the pleasure of using it. They liken literature to a ship and notes that the knowledge of how all parts of a ship are connected does not damage its aesthetic pleasure but enhances the enjoyment of viewing the ship with knowledge of how all its parts were assembled (p. 101). Mohamed et al therefore imply that it is by style that a work of art is assembled and brought to the audience.

Stylistics therefore analyses the different ways (styles) by which the works of art are brought forth (manufactured). We cannot have the novel, a play or poetry without style.

Katie Wales defines stylistics as the study of literary style. He notes that the main aim of stylistics is not just description of the formal features of a text but "to show the functional significance for the interpretation of a text" (p. 437). Wales therefore suggests that literary writers use style to express their subjects and themes. In other words, the reader needs the knowledge of style to interpret and get the author's meaning. Mugubi (2017) defines literary style as the personal and creative fashioning of resources of language by the writer to express his or her ideas (p. 13). To achieve this, the writer has to foreground certain features to make them stand out. The process of foregrounding may violate grammatical rules in what is otherwise referred to as poetic license. It may occur at lexical level in the manner in which the writer chooses words. It may also occur at the Syntactic level- the way he writes his sentences. At a semantic level, writers can use all forms of absurdities and ambiguities, for instance, paradox, oxymoron, pleonasm, and tautology. Writers can even create their own word, otherwise referred to as neologism. A literary writer therefore has at his access diverse language resources that distinguish him from other writers.

6:3 Distinction of Literary Works by Style

Literary scholars world over have defined literature as an art whose medium is the word. Literature is the end product of man's artistic labour and it is therefore absurd to divorce literature from style. Style is an integral part of art. Whereas in language words are symbols of communication, literature employs words to express the beauty of language. William Wordsworth, for instance, defined poetry as the best words arranged in the best order [cited Amateshe (ix)]. The artist chooses linguistic items carefully to express the message in style. A historical or political writer may afford to communicate ordinarily but the literary writer has to remember that style is the soul of art, since literature is art.

Let us look at how Jonathan Swift, Charles Dickens and Ayi kwey Armah, Chinua Achebe, Velma Pollard and Ngugi Wa Thiong'o and other literary writers employed style to transform what would otherwise have been ordinary historical and philosophical works.

When he writes *Gullivers Travels,* Jonathan Swift wants to comment on the political, philosophical and social issues of his times. However, he does not want to make an open, reckless attack on the English society that is vulnerable to censorship. Swift chooses allegory, a style in which whole work is a parable, symbolic and extended metaphor. He writes in parables to attack customs, beliefs, philosophies and odd ideas during the scientific revolution. The choice of allegory distinguishes *Gulliver's Travels* from other sociological and political books of his time.

In Lilliput, Lamuel Gulliver visits a land of short people. Most of the inhabitants are below six inches, the tallest; who also is the king is six inches. The sudden appearance of the huge Gulliver is so shocking that the cabinet convenes to pass legislations on how he will move around town. They label him, the Man Mountain. Gulliver turns out as a security threat in Lilliput. What most astounds him is the king. One inch taller than other subjects, he brags to be 'the tallest man in the universe, 'whose head touches the sun, as a result, he is tyrannical, corrupt and cruel. Gulliver pities the myopia of Lilliputians. He says, "[t]hey see with great exactness but at no great distance," (p. 53), in spite of this, they claim to be at the centre of the universe, no other creatures matter to them.

Swift chooses allegory to satirize his English society. It enables him to attack the pride in his society, particularly emerging philosophies that placed man at the center of creation and looked down on environmental matters. The myopia among Lilliputians suggests that such notions were short sighted since man can only survive in a healthy environment. The tyrannical Lilliputian emperor is King George I who ruled England between 1714 and 1727. The Lilliputian empress is Queen Anne, who blocked Swift's advancement in the Church of England.

Gulliver takes another voyage to Laputa, a country of creatures buried in scientific research to make inventions. They are always in laboratories. The creatures possess bizarre physical features: one eye turned inward and another turned up to the sky. The most stunning thing is that they are so absorbed in their abstract speculation that they cannot see what is going on around them. In Laputa, Swift is using allegory to explore the issue of vanity; he attacks a science that is removed from the realities of life. Being the age of reason, there were scientists who researched for fame rather than making discoveries that solved real life problems.

Gulliver goes to the country of Struldbrugs; in the third part of the novel. Here live immortal creatures some of which are a thousand years old. Struldbrugs do not die but live very miserably: many are deaf, others blind and yet others can only be carried around but still cannot die. By the immortality of struldbrugs, Swift satirizes advocates of immortality during his time: immortality does not mean remaining youthful and happy. As long as aging exists, death is just as good.

Gulliver makes another voyage to the country of houyhnhnms, creatures governed by pure reason. Reason has enabled then to establish a society devoid of poverty and crime; however, they do not have feelings. They lack joy, love and passion. Here, Swift attacks those philosophers who elevated rationality over other parts of the human triangle. Philosophers like Plato described emotions as the primitive part of man and reason the developed part. Swift answers them by use of houyhnhms, that reason alone cannot suffice, human beings need to have feelings.

Gulliver goes to the land of yahoos, lascivious and degenerate creatures that scoff at reason. Swift is attacking those philosophers who emphasized emotional excesses, for example Hobbes. Hobbes observed that life was very short and so humanity should seek pleasure each moment they got. The gluttony of the yahoos gives the author's verdict: Hobbesian philosophy leads to moral depravity.

Similarly, African poets have used allegory to explore issues that affect them in a unique and captivating manner. David Rubadiri uses the thunderstorm to express the effects of the advent of colonialism:

The African Thunderstorm
David Rubadiri

From the West
Clouds come hurrying with the wind
Turning sharply
Here and there
Like a plague of locusts
Whirling
Tossing up things on its tail
Like mad man chasing nothing

Pregnant clouds
Ride stately on its back
Gathering to perch on hills
Like dark sinister wings
The wind whistles by

And trees bend to let it pass
In the village
Screams of delighted children
In the din of whirling wind
Women-
Babies clinging on their backs-
Dart about
In and out
Madly
The wind whistles by
Whilst trees bend to let it pass

Clothes wave like tattered flags
Flying off
To expose dangling breasts
As jiggered blinding flashes
Rumble, tremble and crack
Amidst the smell of fired smoke
And the pelting march of the storm. (Ulli & Moore,1963, p. 170)

The capitalization of 'w' in West in the first line and image of the 'tattered flags' on the last stanza on gives a hint into the allegorical nature of the poem. The West signifies European, colonial powers such as Britain, France, Portugal and 'tattered flag represents the lose of independence. The European powers are likened to a plague of locusts to imply their preparedness to exploit Africa's natural and human resources. 'The pregnant clouds' in the second stanza signifies attributes of Western civilization being brought by Western powers such as Christianity and formal education. The wind signifies the changes being brought by western powers and the trees that give way to the wind are African leaders of that time such as Samore Toure in

West Africa and Lobengula in Zimbabwe. The women represent African societies that are bracing for exploitation. The frantic mood in the last stanza signify the violence that took place during the conquest of African entities (Rumble, tremble and crack/amidst the smell of fired smoke).

Andrew Nyongesa also employs allegory to explore the benefits of the unity of Africa in the *Rise of Rodedom*. Neologism and allegory give this book a special taste compared to other political and historical books. Rodedom is the author's creation (neologism) meaning 'Kingdom of rodents'. The 'kingdom of cats is *Catdom,* which symbolically represents Western Europe. The author writes:

> That immense stretch of land fronting Liondom on the other side of the globe, the vast land in which you found every leaf chivalrous, each flower beautiful, every leaf green; a land with everything in nature prettiest was the 'accursed Rodedom, she was besieged in oceans and seas...rodents with quick wits like hare understood that Rodedom was engrossed in countless questions about the global contempt she suffered. Subsequently, her shape was that of a question mark. (p. 6)

The image of the question mark leads to the conclusion that Rodedom is Africa. And Catdom stands for European empires that scrambled for Africa at the end of the nineteenth century. Therefore Catdom Proper is Great Britain, which in the first chapter they establish their vision and mission for Africa. Angel kittens reveals colonial prejudices towards Africa, "[r]odent is a stupid thief, poor vagabond and confused vagrant... he has no will, he has no conscience, his intellect leaves a lot to desire (2). Leopardom refers to the Germany empire and Witchat I and Nov are emperor Kaiser William and Otto Von Bismark. Foxes are the boers and their infamous apartheid policy in Azania, which is represented by Hedgehoga. Hyanadom represents France and hyenars, autocratic kings like Louis xiv. It is allegory that transforms *Rise of Rodedom* from and ordinary historical work to a work of art.

Charles Dickens employs syntactic style to transform *A Tale of Two Cities* from an ordinary historical and sociological work to a work of art. In the first chapter, he writes:

> It was the best of times, it was the worst of times; it was the age of wisdom, it was the age of foolishness. It was the epoch of belief, it was the epoch of incredulity, it was a season of light, it was a season of Darkness, it was a spring of hope, it was a winter of despair. (p. 13)

Dickens is just introducing a historical novel about Britain and France in the eighteenth century and chooses antithesis to depict the contradictions of this period. Unlike a history work, the absurdity demands that the reader reflects to unearth what the writer means. It was the best of times in Europe because scientific inventions were being made in medicine and military. The industrial revolution had taken root, wealth had been created but it was the worst period because there was the rise of nationalism and Europe was on the brink of revolution and violence. It was the age of wisdom because influential philosophers, scholars and inventors arose, for instance Rousseau, Honore De Balzac, Charles Darwin and Louis Pasteur. Rousseau's ideas challenged the French monarchy. He is remembered for his axiom, "[m]an is born free but everywhere he is in chains." It was the age of foolishness because there rose despotic kings like Louis xiv whose policies oppressed the poor French. The rich did not pay taxes but the poor paid high taxes. His despotism and gluttony provoked the French revolution, which is well depicted in *A Tale of*

Two Cities. The novel is just history retold in syntactic style. Look at the following periodic sentence:

> That they never could lay their heads upon their pillows; that they never could tolerate the idea of their wives laying their heads upon the pillows, that they never could endure the notion of their children laying their heads upon the pillows at all, unless the prisoner's head was taken off. (p. 74)

In this sentence, Dickens wants to say that these characters could not rest until they ensured that 'the prisoner's head was taken off'. But the reader is kept waiting for the main clause at the end of the sentence. Anticipatory clauses precede it to create suspense hence touching our feelings. The periodic sentence distinguishes the novel from a factual historical book.

Simlarly, Joseph Conrad has a knack for syntactic style as is evident in his novel, *Lord Jim*. He chooses the long sentence, which is inconsistent to the demands of grammar. While describing his character, he writes:

> I don't mean inborn courage; I mean just that inborn ability to look temptations straight in the face- a readiness unintellectual enough, goodness knows, but without a pose- a power of resistance, don't you see, ungracious if you like, but priceless- an unthinking and blessed stiffness before the outward and inward terrors, before the might of nature and seductive corruption of men- backed by faith invulnerable to the strength of facts to the contagion of example, to the solicitation of ideas. (p. 38)

Conrad wants to show the bravery of Lord Jim and this is clarified by the main clause at the beginning of the long sentence. Other clauses then follow to expound on the courage for instance, 'blessed stiffness before...terrors, mighty of nature...' This long sentence is technically referred to as a loose paratactic sentence in stylistics defined as a sentence in which the main clause comes at the beginning proceeded by other clauses to emphasize the main clause and create mood. In another instance, Conrad writes,

> He saw himself saving people from sinking ships, cutting away masts from a hurricane, swimming through a surf with a line; or lonely castaway, barefooted and half naked, walking on uncovered reefs in search of shellfish to stave off starvation; Lord Jim confronted savages on tropical shores, quelled mutinies on high seas and on a small boat along the ocean kept up the hearts of despairing men- always an example of devotion to duty, an unflinching as a hero in a book. (p. 11)

Through the skillful use of the sentence, Conrad in the above example distinguishes the use of language in a factual or philosophical book and language use in a novel. Lord Jim's heroic acts are introduced by a main clause: "He saw himself saving people from sinking ships," which is then followed by a dozen clauses that expound and draw our feelings to admire his aspirations and longings in life.

Besides syntactic style, creative writers pay attention to details in their writing to give their work distinction from philosophical and historical works. Whereas the historian will narrates factual events in passing, the novelist will go into details to move the reader's feelings to change their attitude towards the subject. Masuji Ibuse discourages nuclear war by a vivid description of the bombing of Hiroshima. Whereas historians simply mention the bombing of the city and deaths of over fifty thousand people, Ibuse creates the mournful mood that enables the reader to distaste such wars. He writes:

> The injured were crammed in classrooms and sports grounds. The bodies were laid out in a heap at one end of the sports ground. With nightfall, the moans became still and more anguished. Those with brain fever leapt out of the window and started walking through paddy fields. (p. 248)

The mournful mood is further underscored by Iwatake's (the prime mover) assertion that the six hundred casualties that trudged out of Hesaka were "sad shambling procession of ghosts," (251). The details of the destructive power of the bomb stand out in manner uncharacteristic of what we find in history books. While Yasuko is moving around the city after the drop of the bomb, she stumbles on "a corpse clasping a dead baby in its arms" (p. 98) and Yasuko says, "[t]here were bodies along the road completely naked and scorched black, buttocks of each rested in a great pool of faeces. The hair on their heads and elsewhere was burnt; it was only the contours of breasts that could distinguish man and woman" (p. 99). The readers learn a lot more from the bombing of Hiroshima in Ibuse's novel than what they gather from a history book. The historian Walsh Ben narrates the bombing of Hiroshima, "on 6th August 1945 the first nuclear bomb was dropped on Hiroshima by a B-29 bomber and caused appalling damage and horrific casualties. They also left a legacy of cancer and other radiation related diseases," (p. 297). The description is sketchy and the style lacks details like Ibuse's to move our feelings.

Ayi Kwey Armah employs vivid description and lexical deviation to explore his cocerns in independent Ghana thereby distinguishing his works from sociological and historical works. Whereas the ordinary writer steers clear of use of words considered taboo, Armah flouts this convention and uses taboo words in *The Beautiful Ones Are not yet Born*. Although such writers are misconstrued as vulgar, the lexical deviation suggests that Kwame Nkrumah's Ghana is a vulgar society. The novel proceeds with dozens of bizarre descriptions; decadent imagery pervades chapters with details about parts of the human anatomy we cannot mention publicly. In the first chapter, the writer describes the bus as, "choked by rust, rattles along the road in a confused manner... the driver's matches have been spend and he is resigned to his state." The passenger are described as "[s]till bodies walking in their sleep." The cedi note 'emits very old smell, so strong, so very rotten that the stench came with satisfying pleasure (p.3). The conductor for instance, "[s]pits a blob of phlegm on the man's face... the driver also prepares to do the same," (p. 7). With reference to Koomsoon, for example, there is graphic mention of private parts (p. 259), with other taboo words like shit. Armah uses lexical deviation to vent his anger on the political leadership of Nkrumah, that his leadership is vulgar and destitute of moral values. The smelly cedi represents power that corrupts, and the driver and conductor are myopic leaders without a clear vision of where to take the nation. Armah's anger is corroborated by historical records that reveal Nkrumah's excesses just before he is overthrown in 1966. He had promised to introduce in Ghana an economic system that would involve participation of every individual citizen. A few years after independence however he goes against the promises, enriches himself, keeps hundreds of girlfriends and build himself *The Nkrumah Tower* in the capital, Kumasi. Fearing that people would vote out his party, he started appointing people in parliament. The teacher says that the promise had been so beautiful but Komsoon turned against it. In the title, *The Beautiful Ones are not Yet Born*, Armah suggests that if Nkrumah with all his charisma failed to take Ghana to the Promised

Land then the heroes are not yet born. He was a man of different mettle but his failure shocked and disheartened many Ghanaians. By the time he was overthrown, he had fulfilled the axiom, "[a]bsolute power corrupts absolutely."

The African novel is mostly defined by Africanization of language and use of elegant imagery from the African environment. While commenting on the language of African Literature, Achebe writes: "[t]he African writer should be prepared to use English in a way that brings out his message best without altering the language to the extent that its value as a medium of international exchange is lost" (p. 98). The African writer should therefore choose African images such as 'Okonkwo's fame had grown like a bushfire in the Hamattan" (1) in *Things Fall Apart*. The reader is made to wonder why Okonkwo is a bushfire. As the story unfolds, we observe that he is rash, quick and excessively violent. Okonkwo grows into prominence by burning others on the way up. In fact he begins his ascend by throwin Amalinze the cat to the ground in a wresting match. In another instance, Achebe writes, "[t]he drums filled him with fire as it had always done from his youth. He trembled with desire to conquer and subdue" (p. 96). The image of fire signifies Okonkwo's inner energies that would enable him to conquer Umuofia and rise above his father's underachievement.

Other African writers have borrowed Achebe's hybrid strategy in mixing English and African style to distinguish African literature. Nadifa Mohamed used Somali proverbs in her novel, for instance, Ambaro, Jama'a mother tells him, "I know money is like water," (p. 45) to signify the advent of cash economy and its effect on the Somali society. It also foreshadows Jama's blessed life of wealth and influence later in the story.

Mohamed uses Somali words to Africanize her novel to distinguish it from philosophical works. Jama uses the Somali word "hooyo" (p. 45), to refer to his mother to give the novel the African touch. Bride price is referred to using the Somali word "meher" (p. 62), and some ancestral spirits are refered to as "jinnis" (p. 49). Somali religious beliefs and myths are interwoven in the novel to give it a distinction from history and philosophical books. The writer notes that Jama's (the main character) "ancestors had been crow worshippers and sorcerers before the time of the prophet and the people still kept tokens of their paganism" (p. 49). The prophet is a religious allusion to prophet Mohamed, the pioneer of the Islamic religion, which is the Somalis' present religion. Nawal El Saadawi also uses African words to Africanize her stories and hence distinguish her literary works. For instance, she describes Om Saber, one of her female characters as draped in a long "melaya" (p. 91), which is a long loose dress. At weddings, Om Saber would lead "the *yoos yoos* to paint the feet of girls and women with red henna," (p. 92). The "yoos yoos" in this passage suggest Om Sabers female aides. The reader is also informed that Om Saber would carry out abortions with a stalk of *mouloukheya* (ibid), which implies a special stick meant for abortion operations.

Velma Pollard and Ngugi wa Thiong'o use Creole and local dialect to explore issues in their society. Creole signifies a cultural mix that was a consequence of enslavement of African people. Deprived of their African identity the children of freed slaves crafted a language that was mosaic of European and African laguages. Brenda tells Laura that Africans in the United States "treated her like a long lost sister and were ready to care for her" (p. 100). In Pollard (1994), Creole stands out as the language of home- Jamaica. It is in fact the language of the first sentence in the novel. As soon as David (the hero in the novel) arrives in Jamaica from the diaspora, a girl child remarks, "[h]im sick bad," (p. 1). The racism David has undergone in England has caused internal fragmentation to the point of getting a stroke;

nevertheless, David has come home, the place of peace and repose. Pollard suggests that the home cannot be in possession of the English dialect of the oppressor- Queens dialect. It is amazing to realize that both educated and illiterate characters in Pollard's *Homestretch* employ Creole. While conversing with Charley, David says: [w]hen I leave here, Pedro was barely walking, now him is big business. Charley replies, "is a few years well since you leave you know (p. 10).

We notice that the dialect omits auxiliary verbs such as are; the are say "we going" instead of "we are going". It also flouts tenses for instance Charley says, "Jesus turn water into wines." The elite like Laura, the university lectures greets Maas Zee, "[h]ow you do?" and the latter replies, "So, miss Laura, and you?" (93).

A critical study of the novel further reveals the use of linguistic differentiation as a style thereby distinguishing it from a factual story. The author assigns characters language depending on their status in the society. Highly educated characters use Standard English while those in the low society use creole. Brenda and Gerald speak Standard English, for instance, after reaching Jaimaca, at the airport, she tells Laura, "[w]hen you go outside, tell Gerald these damn people are holding me up in here. You know him, don't you?" (52). Later on when Brenda and Laura meet over a snack Brenda uses Standard Dialect to say, "I have a feeling deep down my heart that Jamaica rejected me and gave me what? England and America. And then the few times I have come, this palce seems to be disorganized compared with them..." (88). The Standard Dialect to reveal the in-between space, which Brenda has occupied as a consequence of living in the diaspora. Sometimes Brenda appreciates Jamaica and other times distaste, which is typical of the in-between identity. That is why she uses Creole and Standard Dialect at the same time. Homi Bhabha refers to this type of identity as hybridity- "the unstable element of linkage" (207). At the same time, we find the porter, who belongs to the low class saying, "[f]ix me up no brother," (52). He mean 'now' by 'no'.

In *The River Between,* Ngugi chooses simple idiomatic language and local dialect to explores in his novel. He avoids bombastic tones throughout the novel because he is concerned with the simplicity of the African society before and during the colonial period. The story begins, "[t]he two ridges lay side by side. One was Kameno, the other was Makuyu," (1). Ngugi, through simple idiomatic language, suggests that there was nothing complicated in the traditional African society. The people offered their sacrifices to Murungu, circumcised their children, married, had children and lived in contentment. In other instances, the novelist uses local dialect, which distinguishes the story from a factual, philosophical book. Chege tells his son, Waiyaki, "[g]o then, tell your mother to give you something to put in your mouth," (9). At the sacred grove, he tells Waiyaki, "[t]he roots of this plant are good, when the stomach bites you; boil them in water." (p. 34). Ngugi suggests that the characters speak kikuyu language and so as just like Achebe making an attempt to Africanize the English Language. The existence of the Standard English dialect, local dialect and Kikuyu words such as *thingira* (p. 8) *Gikuyu Karing'a* (p. 66) signify reconciliation, which is the subject of the novel, *The River Between.*

6:4 Stylistics and Oral Literature

Style is is not just a preserve of written literature, but cuts across other genres like Africa folklore. For effective creation of an oral narrative, the creators need to choose relevant aspects of form to express the content effectively.

6:4.1 Style and Oral Narratives

Oral narratives are prose forms of oral literature or African folklore that were narrated by elder to inculcate moral lessons in children. The storyteller had to be creative to effectively depict the intended message. Most African societies had ogre narratives, trickster stories, explanatory tales, dilemma narratives, human tales, fables and spirit tales. In this section, we will briefly look at how style is employed in African oral tales. Let us analyse the following narrative from Nyongesa (2018).

> Long time ago, Nandakaywa, the monster swallowed all the people in the village and left one courageous young man who had built a fort to protect his only sister. Mwambu, the young man, had fierce dogs that barked like thunder whenever the ogre tried to attack. The three dogs, however, protected them on condition that they tasted the food before any human being did. They would not fidget at the enemy if this was disobeyed. Mwambu obeyed this instruction and they lived very long.
>
> One day, Mwambu told his sister that he would travel to a far place for one moon. He therefore told Sela to do as he had always done to be protected from Nandakaywa. The first two days after his departure, Sela obeyed the instruction to the letter. On the third day, she ate the food and then gave it to the dogs. They all refused to eat.
>
> Nandakaywa stormed the fort. Sela raised her pretty face and saw a tall, fat beast with three mouths. He had one round eye at the forehead. His hairy body shook with fury. He roared and picked Sela.
>
> "Dogs, bite him!" Sela cried but it was too late. The dogs hunched at the gate sadly. Nandakaywa seized and swallowed her. When Mwambu returned, he called her sister but there was no response. He ransacked every corner of the fort; her dear sister had

been swallowed by the ogre. He set off to look for Nandakaywa's home. He had swallowed Mwambu's friends, parents and ancestors. Mwambu picked the moon spear, the sun spear and the lightning spear; he walked all the way to the ogre's home. He reached there at sun- up and found young ogres at the gate. He bet they were Nandakaywa's children.

"Where is your father?" he asked.

"On the farm," replied the young ogres.

"Call him, I want Sela!" He ordered.

The young ogre climbed a tree and called in a song:

E papa E papa	Father! Father!
Omwene Sela echile	Sela's owner has come
Namuendebe kaloba	He refused to sit
Namuekindi kaloba	He refused another seat
Balikenye yoo yekamayeye.	He wants your honourable seat.

Nandakaywa heard his son sing and commanded one of his slave ogres to go and check what was amiss at home. Meanwhile, Mwambu speared the son with the moon spear. He collapsed, dead."

When the slave ogre reached home, he got an opportunity to steal the labourer's beer in the house. Upon seeing corpses of the master's sons, he thought they were tipsy and chortled,

"A, ha, ha, ha! These Nandakaywa's are very drunk today! Have you finished the beer?" He greedily ran to steal the beer and Mwambu found an opportunity to kill him.

Mwambu ordered other sons to call the father in futility. They sang the song, he speared them; they sang the song, he speared them. The slave ogres came, they got diverted by the beer; he killed them. Finally, Nandakaywa decided to come. The thump of his feet was the rumble of thunder. *Bwu, bwu, bwu, bwu* thumped his feet. *Rutia,tia..tia..Rutia..tia..tia* ran the sparks from his mouth. He opened his three mouths and growled at Mwambu. The young man did not get scared.

"I want Sela!" He ordered.

The sparks were the only response he got from the ogre, "*Rutia...tia...tia...tia!*"

Mwambu whipped out the moon spear and threw. The ogre opened his mouth and swallowed it. He cast the sun spear. The ogre swallowed it but it blew out one mouth. Mwambu now whipped out the lightning spear.

"No,no,..no!" cried Nandakaywa, "cut this small toe and take all your people."

Mwambu cut the smallest toe of his right foot and the whole village came out. He greeted them very happily and they unanimously made him the chief. That's the end of the story. (Nyongesa, 2018, P. 285- 287).

The story begins with a phrase which is typical of most African oral narratives. The phrase, "Long time ago" is formulaic and is hence referred to as the opening formula. The narrator uses it to transfer the audience from the real world to the world of imagination. It also captures the attention of the audience and introduces the narrator where there are a number of narrators before the audience.

Secondly, there is effective use of characterization. Stylisticians like Mugubi (2017) observe that for effective delivery of content, an artist has to choose relevant aspects of form. (p. 13). The artist in this story chooses Mwambu, Sela, the dogs and ogres to depict the subject of death. Sela's greed wards off the support from those supernatural powers that may protect the family from evil and death. Mwambu stands out as strait laced and thereby prepared to save the community from evil and death.

Thirdly, symbolism stands out as one of the major stylistic features in the story. The artist uses images that represent abstract ideas. Mwambu represents the youth through which society conquers death and extermination. Nandakaywa and the ogres in this story represent death and its determination to exterminate humanity. It only places its hopes in the younger generation that will conquer death through marriage. The dogs signify conditional help from the good spirits, which we forfeit by violating taboos. Those youngmen who succeed like Mwambu are obedient to societal norms. Sela represents greed, recklessness, and its consequences to the society at large.

Another aspect of style is the use of mnemonic features like ideophone, defined as sound words that imitate a movement or create an impression. The artist imitates the sound produced by the ogre, for example, "*Bwu, bwu, bwu, bwu* thumped his feet. *Rutia,tia..tia..Rutia..tia..tia,* ran the sparks from his mouth." The audience perceives the ogres movement and visualizes the ogres' physical capabilities by use of ideophone. The use of song breaks the monotony of narration to bring comic effect in an otherwise melancholic story. The song links the episode of Mwambu's visit to the reappearance of Nandakaywa in the story. It assists in plot development as it brings this story to the climax and resoltion.

The narrator has effectively used plot to express content. Stylisticians define plot as the sequence of events in a story. This story has the introduction where the problem is introduced: Nandakaywa swallows people who eat before the dogs eat. The events get complicated when Sela disobeys the instruction. She is swallowed by Nandakaywa and Mwambu has to look for a solution. The climax is reached during the violent confrontation between Mwambu and Nandakaywa. The conflict is resolved when Nandakaywa releases all the people of Mwambu's village.

There is a dialogue between Mwambu and the ogres to show the gluttonous nature of the ogres. When they come for errands, they get confused by the presence of beer and forget the object of the errand. The artist suggests that excessive consumption of beer has detrimental effect on the society.

The story ends with the formulaic sentence, "That is the end of the story" to transfer the audience from the world of imagination to the real world. It paves the way for the next narrator and leaves the audience to reflect on the story.

6:4.2 Style and Oral Poetry

In traditional Africa songs were one of the prose genres of African folklore. Unlike poems which heavily borrowed the metric pattern of European literature, oral poems have typical features of style that distinguish them. Most songs in traditional Africa are common property of the whole community and none claims their ownership. Look at the example below:

HUNGER
Hunger makes a person climb up to the ceiling
And hold on to the rafters
It makes a person lie down.
But not feel at rest.
It makes a person lie down
And count the rafters.
When the Moslem is not hungry, he says:
"We are forbidden to eat monkey."
When Ibrahim is hungry, he eats baboon!
When hunger beats the woman in the Koinange,
She will run out into the street in daytime.

One who is hungry does not care for taboos
One who is hungry does not care for death
One who is hungry will take
Out of the sacrifice money
Hunger will open it.
"I have filled my belly yesterday"
Does not concern hunger.
We have to sacrifice daily to it. (Anonymous source).

The poem has a number of stylistc devices that not just convey the message, but give it an oralness to appeal to the audience. First is the simplicity of language. The poem has simple English because it is translation from the original language. It could also suggest the simplicity of African culture from which it is derived. There is nothing complicated about traditional African life.

Secondly, there is direct translation or what other stylisticians refer to as local dialect. There are deliberate grammatical mistakes to show that it is the grammar of the mother language, "I have filled my belly yesterday/does not concern hunger." This kind of language use gives the work a local flavour. The audience immediately locates the work of art as African literature since the dialect is distinct. This accounts for the different English dialects that are used in literary works around the world, for example Achebe's Igbo surfeited fiction and Meja Mwangi's use urban slang in the novel.

Furthermore, there are images from the local environment for example, "When Ibrahim is hungry, he eats a baboon." This suggests that there are baboons in this environment and so the artist uses the images to touch the five senses to communicate effectively. African poets and singers have the penchant of drawing images from their environment. A singer from Embu, named Karish sings about a Muthoni of loose morals and enttles the song, *Muthoni Kifagio,* translated as Muthoni the broom. He narrates that the broom sweeps everywhere in the city. He adds that Muthoni is not a personal car but a cab. These images vividly express Muthoni's loose sexual morals as the audience can relate with them in the environment.

Finally, there is use of repetition, which is a common feature of oral poetry. Sentences, phrases and stanzas are repeated to create rhythm in songs. The line "One who is hungry," is repeated to emphasise the demerits of hunger and also bolster the rhythm of the song. Other aspects of rhythm common in African songs are rhyme, assonance, consonance, alliteration, onomatopoeia and ideophone.

6:4.3 Style and Proverbs

Whenever we come across proverbs, we are more interested in the content, but forget that there is the manner by which the message is conveyed. There is no literature without how what is conveyed to the audience. It is style that makes it possible for the proverb to convey that message. Look at the following African proverbs:

Nandakambila kakonela khumwanda kwenjoli is a Luhya proverb translated as a person who does not heed advice is on the path of death. The strength of this proverb is in the sound effect in its mother tongue. The repetition of the /a:/ sound is assonace, which gives it poetic appeal. Similarly, the repetition of /k/ is consonance to create rhythm for emphasizing the message. The artist knows that a message should be embellished in a captivating form to communicate effectively.

The second Luhya proverb, *enyungu yatekha namasaka sewechangamo bululu tawe* is translated to, "A pot that cooks bitter vegetables does not lose its bitter taste." (Nyongesa, 2012, p. 87). It means that when someone gains good experience, he becomes wise and will never disappoint. The speaker uses metaphor because the pot represents the elders who have the experience and the youth should be loyal to learn as much as they can. Bitterness represents the challenges of life that the elder have overcome to become wise. Therefore, there is symbolism in the proverb.

The third proverb is the Somali proverb *abdiboolan wa dhab* translated as a silent mouth is gold (Nyongesa, 153). The speaker compares a silence to gold and so there is use of metaphor. If we want to know the value of silence, we should just behold the worth in gold. The proverb in the first language has mnemonic features. The repetition of /a:/ on the three words brings assonance in the proverb to give it a poetic appeal. The /b/ is also repeated on the first and last word to create consonance, which is musical.

The next proverb is a Kiswahili one: c*hurururu si ndo ndo ndo*, translated as the gushing sound of water is not the dropping sound of it. The first sound imitates the the splashing of water and the second imitates the dropping sound of water. These are sound words that imitate the movement and are just created by the speaker. There is therefore the use of ideophone to convey the message in the proverb.
The last proverb is a Somali proverb, *kura jire, kaa jire* translated as he pretends to be with us but he is not with us (Nyongesa 2012, p.79). The mother tongue version of the proverb contains mnemonic effects to convey the message effectively. There is repetition of the word "Jire" to make proverb musical thereby emphasizing the message. The sound /k/ is repeated in the first position bringing in alliteration for poetic appeal. Repetition of the /a:/ in the form is assonance to make the proverb musical. Attempt a stylistic analysis of the following proverbs:

i).Family names are like flowers, they blossom in clusters.

ii) He devoured kaffir beer and it devoured him.

iii) The prodigal cow threw away her tail.

iv) He milks also cow heavy with calf.

v). Kill the warrior and give him his rights.

vi) Navaloga killed a buffalo.

vii) Asiyesikia la mkuu huvunjika guu
   The person who does not heed the alder's advice breaks his limb

viii) Kamalwa Kakhinia emboe
   Beer makes the tethered cow dance

ix) The violent elephant never preserves its tusk.

x).Sibala engara
   The world is a rim.

6.5 Conclusion

This chapter set out to analyse the role of stylistics theory in distinguishing a work of art from a philosophical, sociological, political and historical work. It was interesting to note that style is indeed the distinguishing factor between a historical book and a novel. Although there were writers who wrote about the plight of the industrial and French revolutions in Europe, Dickens stands out because of his style in *A Tale of Two Cities*. It was also amazing to look at the captivating manner in which Swift addresses the challenges of his generation using allegory in *Gullivers' Travels*. Caribbean and African Literature have also been defined by unique style that involves a mix of European and African Language forms. It is evident that stylistics, like other theories, traverses all genres of literature from written forms such as the novel and poetry to unwritten genres such as oral narratives, songs and proverbs. There can be no literature without style.

REFERENCES
Achebe, Chinua (1958). *Things Fall Apart*.London: Heinmann Publishers.
Achebe, Chinua (1975). The African Writer and English Language. In *Morning Yet Creation on Creation Day*. Doubley: Anchor Press.
Amateshe, A., D. (1989).*Introduction to East African Poetry*. Narobi: East African Publishers.
Armah, A. K. (1968).*The Beautiful ones Are not yet Born*. London: Heinneman.
Bhabha, H. (1994).*The Location of Culture*. London: Routledge.
Conrad, J. (1900). *Lord Jim*. London: Penguin Popular Classics.
Dickens C. (1858).*A Tale of Two Cities*.Penguin Popular Classics. London.
Ibuse M. (1969).*Black Rain*. New York and Tokyo:Kodasha International.
Khattak, M., Menaz a & Khatak I. (2012). Role of Stylistics in Interpreting Literature. *City University Research Journal 3*: P. 10-15.
Mohamed, N. (2010).*Black Mamba Boy*. London: HerperCollins Publisher.
Mugubi, J. (2017). Style in Literature. Nairobi. Royallite Publishers.
Nyongesa A. (2012). Worms in the Lounge. Nairobi. Splendour Publication Agencies.

Nyongesa A. (2013). *Rise of Rodedom*. New York: Raider Publishing International.
Nyongesa A. (2018). *The Water Cycle*. Chitugwiza. Mwanaka Media and Publishing.
Simpson, P. (2004). *Stylistics; a Resource Book for Students*. London and New York: Routledege.
Swift J. (1726).*Gullivers Travels*. London: Penguin Popular Classics.
Thomas K., Leornard P. (Eds). (1965). *Writing Prose*. London: Oxford University Press.
Ngugi W. T. (1965).*The River Between*.Nairobi: EAEP.
Wales, K. (2001).*A Dictionary of Stylistics*. Harlow: Longman.
 Walsh, B. (1996) GCSE *Modern World History*. London: Hodder Murray.
Windowson H. G. (1975).*Stylistics and the Teaching of Literature*. London: Longman.
Pollard, V. (1994) *Homestretch*. Kingston: Longman Carribean Writers.
Ulli B. &Gerald M.(Eds).(1963).*Penguin Book of Modern African Poetry*. London: Penguin Group.

CHAPTER SEVEN:

PHILOSOPHY AND CONTEMPORARY AFRICAN EXPERIENCE

7.1 Introduction

Many Africans relegate philosophy in lecture halls and fail to see it as wisdom that may improve the quality of their lives. Vladmir Lenin and Julius Nyerere got surfeited by teaching socialist ideas and practically applied these ideas to their communities. Although communism failed in the two nations, it was an attempt to apply theory in our contemporary lives. Psychoanalytic principles have been applied the world over in treatment of mental problems in contemporary life. Feminism has been applied in many societies today by persuading governments to implement affirmative action for girls and women. In Kenya today, the constitution reserves fourty seven seats for women to represent women and girls in parliament. But to what extent should radical feminism be applied given that it originated from the West? African thinkers have questioned blind application of radical feminism to the African situation. Postcolonialism has been practiced in many African countries with return to African culture rejection of wetern values. Literature was highly affected by Africans rejecting the writing of African literature in European languages. But there are philosophers who argue that total rejection of foreign culture is not a solution to the current mosaic world where cultures mix through education and migration. This chapter will explore some philosophical concepts, analyse their benefits to the African society and interrogate the crevices in others. The author will focus on postcolonialim and feminism. The ideas Frantz Fanon, Edward Said, Homi Bhabha, Stuart, Gyatri Spivak and Chandra Mohanty will form the basis of our argument. The central question is whether Africa will be better or worse if these philosophical ideas are implemented by the leadership in power. Apart from Marxism, other philosophical ideas such as hybridity and national culture have been ignored by most African leaders.

7.2 Cultural Essentialism: A Sordid Boon at the Shores of Sub-Saharan Africa

In our Gikuyu tradition, it is the lead woman who urges the husband to marry again. "Get me a companion." […] The management of a polygamous household is a matter of individual liberty. Each woman has her own hut…entirely under her own control. When age set peers visit, the wives exercise their freedom, which amounts to something like polyandry. Each wife is free to choose anyone among the age group and give him accommodation for the night. (Kenyatta, 1938, P. 181)

The above quote from Jomo Kenyatta's book underscores the passion with which most independent leaders in Africa desired for a return to past traditions and culture. From Leopold Senghor in Senegal to Aime Ceisar, the clarion call was the rejection of foreign culture and a return to a lost past to restore the African person. At this time, it is probable that none of them realized that the fixed identities they elevated would arm Africans with the much needed arsenal to fight each other. A few years after independence, ethnic conflicts arose as consequence of cultural difference. Favouritism of people of certain ethnic communities in government appointments, employment in companies and promotions in places of work became norms. Today, political mobilization is ethnic- based the competition of which degenerates to violent factions that destroy the social fabric of these nations. Ethnicity is politicized and politicians return to their people to form a formidable base before they seek support from other ethnicities in the country. In the event of allegations of corruption leveled against a politician, members of his community rally behind them. Vernacular media stations behind the mask of promoting African languages and culture perpetuate hate against those communities perceived as enemies to the privileged community. Okogu and Omudjere (2002) observe that tribal groups in African terrain have different cultures with different ideologies with inherent discrimination that evolve series of wars and terrorism (94). They therefore suggest that any tendency to encourage diversity exposes these nations to hostility and political strife.

Soon after independence, African nations resolved to go back to their past cultures. Africanization programmes were introduced to restore African identities that colonialism had destroyed. African leaders of the time were inspired by Negritude Movement to hate everything Western and glorify anything African. Literary and political writers encouraged Africans to return to their culture. Kenyatta (1938) in his work *Facing Mount Kenya* attacks western culture and encourages his people to return to their past traditions. The book has sections of initiation, kinship, marriage, traditional religion and magic. The final chapter insists on unity and integration of Gikuyu life. The chapter on initiation gives graphic details and ethnic justification of female genital mutilation. The chapter on marriage defends polygamy as aforementioned in the abstract. Unlike Nyerere who writes to defend the ways of Tanzanians, Kenyatta's work defends the interests of one ethnic community: Agikuyu. In her review of the book, Celarent Barbara writes:

The powerful critical passages, sometimes angry, sometimes wry-surface when Kenyatta's forbearance has been exhausted and ethnographic detachment disappears into Gikuyu passion. I should underscore that the passion is first and foremost Gikuyu, not African. It is his tribe and its practices that Kenyatta discusses and defends here, not African customs in general. He only mentions the Masai...he had Masai ancestors. (723)

Ensnared in the colonial divisive policies, most African leaders at this time could not discover that such tendencies indirectly perpetuated colonial legacy. The more steeped African communities remained in their traditions, the more divided and weaker the continent would be, and a weaker Africa would be a fertile ground for neocolonialism. Literary writers picked the thread to glorify Africa's past. Negritude poets denounced anything Western and lauded even every aspect of African civilization. In the Poem, "New York," Senghor writes:

> New York! At first I was confused by your beauty, by those great golden long legged girls
> so shy at first before your blue metallic eyes, your frosted smile
> so shy...two weeks without rivers or fields, all the birds of the air falling
> sudden and dead on the high ashes of flat roof tops. (318)

The poem reveals Negritude's rejection and spite for anything Western. The white girls are "long legged" and therefore ugly to the persona; their eyes are blue but "metallic," which suggests that they have no human feelings. Their smile is far from warm; it is "frosted" instead. New York has no fields and rivers like Sub Saharan Africa and extreme pollution is a death sentence to the birds. Playwrights and novelists also elevated African tradition. Francis Imbuga in *Burning of Rags* romanticizes the beauty of Luhya culture and condemns the modern intelligentsia embodied in Denis Agala for abandoning aspects of African culture such as circumcision. Although in *Aminata* Imbuga attempts to raise the position of women, the heroine's failure to inherit land at the end of the play shows the playwright's reverence for African tradition.

When it came to the language of African literature, those with a weak spot for cultural essentialism sanctioned the use of African vernaculars in writing true African Literature. Ngugi Wa Thiong'o, for example, had set himself against the use of foreign languages in African Literature. With Obi Wali and Chinweizu, they proposed that African writers should write literature in African languages to ensure that literature is connected to a people's revolutionary struggle against colonialism. For them, the use of African languages would make African writers dangerous to colonial powers because they are directly speaking to the people but writing in European languages, would be crippling. Ngugi holds that language was at the centre of imperialism. In his work, *Decolonizing the Mind*, he notes that whereas the bullet was the means of physical subjugation, language was the means of spiritual subjugation (p. 9).

Nonetheless, there were writers who opted for the middle ground. Christopher Okigbo was one the most talented hybrid poets whose work is steeped in mythologies of Asia, Europe and rural Igbo. Robert Fraser describes him as poet of "[w]ide and voracious reading in literatures if Greece and Rome," (p. 177). For him to be a writer was to partake in an international community of letters, not being narrowed down to Igbo culture in Nigeria. He therefore rejected what Bhabha terms as 'fixity and fetishness of identity' (p. 9). In this connection, Okigbo turned down a prize at the first festival of black arts in Dakar, Senegal because he did not consider himself exclusively as an African writer. He did not embrace negritude because he thought it was just too simplistic. "It's not that I dislike it," he said, "it is because when you have read a lot of it, you begin to have the feeling that it is so easy to do it." Okigbo's poetry was therefore a departure from that of Okot P' Bitek and Leopold Senghor. K.L. Godwin (1964) observes that Okigbo constructs poems following European musical compositions in a series of movements with themes, developments, repeats and reminiscences.

7:3 Postcolonialisn and the African Experience

Should philosophical ideas not be applied to our African experiences? Should such ideas just remain in analysis of books? Philosophy as Kwasi Wiredu explains can assist in day to day lives of Africa. In this subsection, the author will discuss postcolonialism and how it can correct anomalies in African societies. The following concepts of postcolonial theory are invaluable in analysis of cultural essentialism in Africa:

7:3.1 Orientalism

The Creation of Binary Opposition

In his work, *Orientalism*, Said (1977) observes that European orientalist scholars divided the world by creation of two binary factions: the occident and the orient. That the occident is the West and comprises of the Europeans and the orient is the East, comprising of Arabs, Chinese and Japanese.

Skewed Definition

Orientalist scholars, according to Said, construct the factions as different within the perimeter of their knowledge. They create the West and East as fixed unequal blocs. They construct the West as strong, rational, humane and powerful as opposed to the East that is weak, cruel, irrational and sexually unstable. He writes:

> Europe is powerful and articulate. Asia is defeated and distant. It is Europe that articulates the orient, this articulation is a prerogative not of puppet master, but of a genuine creator whose life giving power represents the otherwise silent and dangerous space beyond familiar boundaries. The orient insinuates danger. Rationality is undermined by Eastern excesses. (p. 57)

Expounding Said's ideas, Meyda (2001) observes that by using diverse works from literary, scientific and historical disciplines, orientalist scholars draw a distinction between the West and the East, of which knowledge they used to subjugate the East (p. 17).

Orientalism is invaluabe to this study because by creation of West/East, strong/weak; superior/inferior, civilized/backward; chaste/sensual, rational/sentimental factions, orientalist scholars posited a polarity or duality that is typical of cultural essentialism, a strategy of political mobilisation in African nations. Orientalism is an essentializing discourse same as NASA/JUBILEE political formations we find in Kenya. Said implies that the two factions, created by orientalists are static and distinct hence in an eternal state of tension devoid of any prospect of peace. The minorities, viewed as inferior and 'backward', seclude themselves from the dominant group that drool in a false image of superiority, strength and rationality thereby polarizing the host nation.

7:3.2 Nationalism

Colonialism Destroys National culture

Fanon (1963), looks at national culture in new independent nations. He observes that colonialism, steeped in prejudices, erodes national culture after centuries of colonial exploitation. It becomes a conglomeration of behavioural patterns and creativity and passion are eradicated (p. 172).

Creation of National Culture

The leaders of independent nations should embark on creation of national culture. Fanon defines national culture as all efforts made by people to describe and improve their situation via thoughtful selection of practices that will bolster their existence (p. 168). During the formation of national culture the new leaders should work in step with the people to shape the future. They should not reject those new practices and customs that the people have opted for.

National Culture is not African Culture

Fanon emphasizes that in their efforts to create national culture, revolutionaries and native intellectuals should not relive precolonial past. National culture does not mean a return to precolonial traditions and so leaders should not concentrate efforts on resuscitating traditions to erect a tradition similar to negritude with a delusion to dicover a people's aspirations. He writes, "[n]ational culture is no folklore where an abstract populism is convinced it has uncovered the popular truth. It is not some congealed mass of noble gestures, in other words less and less connected with the reality of the people," (168).

Fanon's concept of nationalism is beneficial to this paper since it expounds on cultural essentialism and true nationalism, which are subjects in this study. That the creation of national culture should not be a license to embrace cultural fixity. His refusal to return to precolonial traditions is a warning against cultural essentialism, which will proceed contrary to the people's wishes. That the people, who have fought for liberation, have created a new platform to create a national culture and so the leaders should be careful to work "in step with the people," (168). At this point, Fanon refers to cultural hybridity since the people desire to adopt that which is good from the modern ways of life. He asserts that African leaders that are still striving for African culture will do no more than compare coins and sarcophagi. Fanon lays the foundation of cultural hybridity and true nationalism.

7:3.3 Cultural Fixity

Hall (1990) comes up with models of cultural identity that define transition of identity of the Caribbean populace. First, he postulates the traditional model that views identity in terms of one shared culture, hiding inside the many. Hall refers to it as artificial for cultural values are imposed on people because they share a history and ancestry. Citing the Caribbean example, Hall asserts that Caribbeans use this model to seek rediscovery of identity in Africa given their African origin (393). He likens this to what Frantz Fanon calls "passionate research," (393). Hall points out that such identity was crucial in postcolonial struggles but is not relevant in the contemporary, cosmopolitan world.

Bhabha (1988) expounds on the concept of cultural fixity. He observes that fixity is a barrier to positive change. Referring to Fanon, he stresses that perpetual insistence on past traditions hinders transformation. He asserts that Fanon's metaphor that the people are in "[f]luctuating movement of occult instability," is not plausible without acknowledging the third space (p. 9-23). The 'flactuating movement' for Bhabha refers to the peoples desire to hybridize the values with emerging changes in science and technology, which will remain a mirage if they choose the path of cultural fixity. The leaders of the independence movements are the torch bearers of hybridity where they spearhead cultural exchanges and transformation of people into mutants. At the third space, Bhabha holds that there is no stagnation. He gives the example of Algeria, a people's traditions only protected them against colonialism. After the struggle for independence, they are free to establish a new national culture by hybridisation. Those native intellectuals who want to return the people to precolonial traditions should brace for disappointment because during the struggle Algerians, "[d]estroyed continuities and constancies of the nationalist tradition.They are now free to negotiate and translate their national identities," (9-23). Cultural fixity is central to this study as it sheds light to the true meaning of cultural essentialism, which is the subject of this paper.

7:4 Said's Orientalism and the African Reality

Most African leaders after independence underscored cultural essentialism in the guise of celebration of their cultural heritage. African communities returned to their traditional cultures to distinguish themselves from each other. Knowledge of differences emerged as ethnic communities interacted. As a result, they began to realize weaknesses in each other's cultural practices. The Luo perpetuation of non circumcision contrasted with Kikuyu emphasis of the rite and within no time the two cultures stood in binary opposition. Those communities that circumcise men start seeing themselves as superior to others. Said asserts that the two factions are in constant state of tension as one community views itself as more superior to the other. In Andrew Nyongesa's *The Endless Battle* there exist Bantu communities and Somali in a binary opposition. Somali characters think they are better than Bantus and Nilotes because of their curly hair and the islamic religion. Eugene, the prime mover is shocked at the otherness prevalent in the Somali society. Bantus and Nilotes are called names: *Ngurale, mathomatho, adhon,* derogatory words that describe their tufty hair and black skin. The cause of the tension between the Somali and the Bantus is the desire to glorify own culture and refusal to appreciate the Other. Eugene refuses to integrate in the dominant Somali culture while Somalis likewise reject the incoming novelties that Christian immigrants bring. Extreme love for one's culture which most Africans see as the back bone of patriotism is the embodiment of orientalism, an essentializing discourse that propagates tribalism in Africa.

Julius Nyerere foresaw the rise of cultural essentialism in his country and proceeded to prevent it. He referred to it as "ideologisation and politicisation of tribe" that was poised to hinder the buiding of new nation states in Africa. He insisted that the new African nations had to weave together nations out of tribes and ethnicity of which orientalist discourses were a barrier. When in 1991 he was questioned as to why he saw tribal identities as inherently negative when he himself is a proud Mzanaki, he replied:

> I am a good Mzanaki, but I won't advocate a Kizanaki-based political party. So I am a Tanzanian, and of course I am Mzanaki. Politically I'm a Tanzanian, culturally I'm Mzanaki (p. 2).

How many nations in Africa followed Nyerere's contempt for orientalist tribal mobilisation? On the contrary many adopted the Negritude stance that ideologised and politicied the tribal identities. Everything African was beautiful: everything from the West was ugly. Anything from the self is beautiful: everything from the Other is ugly. Read the following extracts from the poems of Okot P' Bitek:

> You kiss her on the cheek
> As white people do
> You kiss her open sore lips
> As white people do
> You suck slimy saliva
> From each other's mouths
> As white people do (p. 53).

The self, a diehard of African culture, casts aspersions at kisses just because he feels that it came form the West. He uses a macabre tone to describe it, for instance, "suck slimy saliva/ from each other's mouths". Should a deep kiss be obnoxious for the sheer reason that Europeans were the first to use it in Africa? The self proceeds:

> Butter from cows milk
> Or the fat from edible rats
> Is cooked with *likura*
> Or itika
> You smear it on your body
> And the aroma
> Lasts until next day. (p. 68)

In the above instance, he dismisses European body lotions and advocates a return to traditional oil made "cows milk" and "fat from edible rats". The persona seems to be speaking out of personal vendetta for the West rather than reason. The audience wonders how wrong it is to buy a more convenient body lotion from a modern industry. He now shifts to another aspect:

> I confess
> I do not deny
> I do not know
> How to cook like a white woman
> I cannot use the primus stove
> I do not know how to light it
>
> Electric fire kills people
> They say
> It is lightning
> They say
> The white man has trapped
> And caught the rain cock
> And imprisoned it

The self refuses to use modern cookers and prefers the parochial cooking stones. He rejects the electric cooker because it exposes him to electric shocks and does not know how to light the kerosene stove. The reasons given for the rejection are terribly flimsy and unconvincing. Look at the poem below:

Viral Attitudes
Andrew Nyongesa

> I live in the north: you live in the south,
> like North Pole and South Pole,

We cannot meet.

I have curly hair: you have tuft hair,
like goat and sheep,
We cannot meet.

You eat pork: I hate pork,
like gentiles and Jews,
We cannot meet.

I have smooth skin: you have rough skin,
Like hippo and crocodile,
How can we meet, midget?

I live on the mountain: you live near the lake,
like China and Japan,
How can we be same?

I am a farmer: you keep livestock,
like Cain and Abel,
How can we meet?

I am brown: you are blue black,
Like G and Boy blue,
How can we be same?

I am many: you are few,
Like the Allies and the Axis
How can you fight me?

I am wise: you are foolish,

like Hare and Hyena
How can we be same? (Nyongesa, 2013, 67)

The self in the poem above expresses his self importance over the Other. He views his culture as better than the other. Their land, their hair, the complexion and population are better than the other. This poem depicts the actual demerits of cultural essentialism to a society. Said's concept is brought to the ground, the self bragging of her wisdom while the Other is foolish. While cultural essentialism was pertinent in the fight against colonialism, it becomes destructive in the building of nation states in Africa. After independence, African communities turned hostility against Western culture to other African cultures. The result was dilapidation of the national fabric, particularly with the emrgence of tribal political formations in Rwanda, Kenya, Somalia, South Sudan and Uganda. The failure to appreciate anything in the Other will no doubt erect Said's Orient and Occident within an African nation. In Rwanda, the Hutu/Tusi essentalializing discourse degenerated into bloody genocide after which nearly one million lives were lost. The tribal, political formations, Party of National Unity and Orange Democratic Movement in Kenya led to expulsion of Agikuyu from the Rift Valley following a polarizing election in 2007. Other ethnicities rallied behind ODM against the Agikuyu (PNU) because of the love for their culture and language. There were many complaints about their tendency to start estates in foreign lands with names from their mother culture. Boubock and Faist (2010) refer to this aspect of cultural essentialism as the concept of iconography, where diaspora preserve symbols of their culture, for example, churches, mosques, synagogues, theatres, sports clubs, conference rooms, monuments and other elements that perpetuate memory of the motherland (38). They observe that it is iconography that enables diaspora not to be diluted into the host society, and so maintain their distinct identity. This distinct identification makes the diaspora more vulnerable to hostility by the host community. It emphasizes *difference*, which creates a duality with the host community. While cultural essentialism was appropriate for the struggle for freedom, it is an eyesore for nationalism in many African countries. Appiah (1992) observes that "for political purpose of acquiring independence after experiencing European colonialism, Pan-Africanists articulated themselves with their shared African ancestry to build their racial and political solidarity" (p. 32). Pan-Africanists emphasized the beauty of African race and culture, a type of national pride that pitted African civilization against Western civilization in colonies hence a recipe for armed conflicts. It would however be absurd to perpetuate cultural essentialism in a cosmopolitan African nation.

7:5 Fanon's National Culture and the African Quandary

Fanon (1963) defines national culture as all efforts made by people to describe and improve their situation via thoughtful selection of practices that will bolster their existence (p. 168). National culture, for Fanon, is not traditional African rituals and ways of thinking, but those new and old practices that the people opt to have after independence. The choice of food, old and new; the choice of rites of passage, old and new; the choice of national language; the choice of behaviour patterns, old and new. Fanon cautions the independent leaders to move "in step" with the people to avoid the danger of being left behind in quest of modernity. National culture does not mean a return to precolonial traditions and so leaders should not concentrate efforts on resuscitating traditions to erect a tradition similar to Negritude with a delusion to dicover a people's aspirations.

Fanon therefore casts doubt on the ability of cultural essentialism to establish strong and united African nations. Western culture had already made its impact on the African continent in matters of education, medicine, engineering, religion, mode of dress and much more and it would be delusional to make an obsolute return to what Hall (1990) refers to as the traditional model. He therefore urges Africans to create some sort of hybrid culture by inculcating values from within and without. The choice of Kiswahili as a national language in Tanzania contributed greatly to the creation of a cohesive nation. Achebe (1975) echoes Fanon's ideas in his contribution to the language best suited to African Literature. He observes that colonialism left the language of communication. Africa has more than two thousand languages and it would be very difficult for readers to understand literature if it was written in vernaculars (p. 98). Most scholars agree that emphasis on vernaculars will underscore the ethnic divide that already haunts African societies. The more different societies become, the weaker the social fabric, which was the desire of British colonialists in Africa. Weber (2009) observes that ethnic animosities existing in Kenya today can be traced back to the adminstrative approach used by colonial rulers. He writes:

> Although the two countries were at one point colonized by the British, colonialists' attention was focused on Kenya as the centre of East African development. Measures were taken to build up a strong Agricultural export sector that involved exproriation of Kenyan farmers and prevention of Kenyan communities to unite against colonialism. British administration in Kenya followed "divide and rule" policy. British rulers set out to divide the population and create ethnically homogeneous entities. Through this policy formerly fluid and contextual ethnic identities were frozen and tribes deliberately invented. (11)

Weber reinforces Fanon's rejection of the return to African traditional culture to evade the temptation of sliding back to the divisive existence of the colonial era. The British colonilists knew that the more steeped Kenyan communities were in their cultures, the more distant they would be from each other. Ogot (2005) notes that the aim was to create "self sufficient closed static and homogeneous linguistic and ethnic units" (p. 267). Ogot's use of the term static is a reference to Said's orientalism. The two factions created by cultural essentialism are fixed and in a binary opposition. Ogot notes that Meru tribe was deliberately invented to underscore otherness and subsequent division in the African society.

They combined Tigania, Igembe, Imenti, Miutini, Igoji, Mwimbi and Muthambi into Meru ethnic group and settled Europeans in between neighbouring ethnic entities to prevent inter ethnic co-operation. (ibid)

Ogot's claims suggest that African communities co-existed quite peacefully and united in the precolonial era. Communities that had similar language patterns lived in unity and intermarried to forge ties that were benevolent to the two sides. The advent of colonialism planted a wedge among them, for instance Agikuyu, Embu, Meru and Akamba. The British oppressors emphasized the need to stick to one's community and culture to retain a weak social fabric to facilitate easy conquest and domination. It would therefore be absurd for African leaders today to perpetuate such legacy. Weber writes:

> The creation of closed and cut off ethnic units enabled the British colonialists to effectively rule the Kenyan population without having to fear a united resistance. Attempts of Kenyans to organize a cross-ethnic resistance, for example in the East African Association, were immediately banned by the colonial rulers stating that they would only allow an association with members from one

ethnic group. Through the prohibition to organize nationally, the Kenyan population was left with the option to develop locally restricted ethnic associations (Chweya, 2002; p.91). Thereby, ethnic nationalism was encouraged and the foundation for today's ethnic representation in politics sowed by the British administration. (p. 11)

These divisions have continued in Kenya today, with the rise of vernacular radio and television stations that some communities use to insult other communities to destroy national consciousness. Prior to the 2007 general election, Kass FM, a Kalenjin based radio station was allegedly involved in inciting one community against another. Contrary is the case in Tanzania where the Germans used a less vigorous approach that allowed for hybridity of sorts. Tripp (1999) observes that although they maintained homogeneous units, the communities were governed by *Maakidas*- well educated Muslims from the coast that spoke Kiswahili (38). Their use of Kiswahili inspired many Tanzanians to start to abandon their traditional cultures and appreciate other communities. Jerman (1997) contends that when the British took over Tanganyika to administer it on behalf of the League of Nations, they rejected *Maakidas* because "they accelerated the disintegration of tribal customs". Progressive administrators like Charles Dundas broke away from ethnic based administrative boundaries and called for regional policies rather than the scientifically advocated creation of tribes (p. 227).

With these different colonial legacies, Kenya and Tanzania took different trajectories after independence. Mwalimu Julius Nyerere found it simpler to tend a national consciousness given that Dundas and maakidas had laid the foundation of hybridity. Tanzania birthed a national culture with Kiswahili as the official and national language. Vernaculars were discouraged in offices and business premises

(Weber, 2009, 18). The president himself spoke the language in his home and statehouse. He discouraged ethnic consciousness and united Tanzania in one strong nation. In Kenya:

Experts stress that Kenya's first President Kenyatta sometimes addressed the population in his mother tongue, Kikuyu even if people did not belong to the Kikuyu ethnic group and hence were not able to understand him (Appendix B4, Kenya, 2.). In addition, the liberalization of the media in 2002 and the spread of vernacular radio stations, such as Inooro FM and Kameme FM (Kikuyu ethnic group), and Kass FM (Kalenjin ethnic group), is seen to pronounce the use of vernaculars and thereby to increase ethnic consciousness and animosity (Wamwere, 2008; p.41). In the post-election period, these radio stations provided a platform for hate-speeches and thereby crucially contributed to the ethnic violence experienced in 2008. (p. 18)

The use of vernacular by the leader distances other ethnic groups because as Ngugi asserts, language transmits the culture of that community to others who may be unwilling to learn it. Such an action is also an attempt to make one ethnic community ineligibly superior to the rest. It therefore encouraged other Kenyan communities to compete with Kikuyu by nurturing their own languages. It became apparent after liberalization of the media during the Mwai Kibaki era (2002- 2012). Many radio stations sprang up throughout Kenya some of which entrenched national disintegration. Steeped in their traditions, most Kenyan communities view other ethnic groups as the Other and it can easily degenerate to violence. There is talk of the Kikuyu nation, Luhya nation, Luo nation, Akamba nation, Somali nation living in one place, Kenya. Is the Kenyan dream real? Is national integration plausible? Is this a celebration of diversity of a celebration of disintegration?

Political mobilization is purely ethnic and so the competition between different ethnic groups degenerates to political violence. Halakhe (2013) observes that ethnic protagonists have abused Kenya's voting rules to influence the outcome of elections. He writes:

> Because Kenyans must cast a ballot in a location where they had registered to vote, one strategy is to incite violence to displace "outsiders" who base on their ethnicity votes for certain candidates. (p. 7)

"Outsiders" tag is the reference to otherness, which is the essence of cultural essentialism. Fanon warns that cultural fixity underscored by Negritude is not national culture. He writes: "[n]ational culture is no folklore where an abstract populism is convinced it has uncovered the popular truth. It is not some congealed mass of noble gestures, in other words less and less connected with the reality of the people," (p. 168). The cultural populism in most African nations is enhanced by the media. The untrained journalists in vernacular radio stations flout the code of ethics of journalism to incite violence among communities. Oyaro (2008) in his report writes, "[t]he ethnic hate our radio stations were propagating about those outside their community was unbelievable. The unfortunate thing is we let these callers speak vile and laughed about it". The Other laughs at the insults of the self because Otherness is entrenched in this society. The habit of cherishing one's own and disparaging the other is so common place that taking offence is not just self destruction, but an exercise in futility. Fanon foresaw the possibility of cultural essentialism (propagated by Negritude) politicizing ethnicity in African nations. Those nations that ignored his ideas took this bearing and do experience political animosity in most electoral seasons. Halakhe observes that electoral violence in Kenya stems from politicisation of ethnicity (p. 6).

7:6 Bhabha's Hibridity and the Ethnic Divide in Africa

Bhabha (1994) observes that sticking to past histories and cultures would bring about dangers of fixity and fetishism of identities (p. 9), and it would deny people insight into experiences beyond the borders. He writes:

> Fanon recognizes the crucial importance for subordinated peoples asserting their indigenous cultural traditions and retrieving their repressed histories. But he is far too aware of the dangers of fixity and fetishism of identities within the calcification of colonial cultures to recommend that roots be struck in the celebratory romance of the past by homogenizing the history of the present. (p. 9)

In this text, Bhabha suggests that cultural fixity is asserting past traditions and reliving repressed histories. It lauds fixed identities and denounces mixed ones, which is a threat to national cohesion in Africa. This was witnessed in Rwanda when the colonialists and post independent government perpetuated traditions that pitted one culture against the other. During the pre-colonial era, the Rwandese had a monarchy that was socially stratified in league with the cultural differences. At the top of the social stratum were the Tutsi, followed by Tutsi Banyaruguru, Tutsi Hima, and then Hutu at a lower cadre and the Twa at the very bottom. Uvin (1999) writes:

> Colonialists acted through the kings to reinforce the stratification... the colonizers reserved education and jobs almost

exclusively for the Tutsi. By the 1950s thirty one of the thirty three Africans in the legislative body were Tutsi. Five hundred and forty four of five hundred and fifty nine sub chiefs were Tutsi... political, social and even economic relations became more rigid, unequal and biased against the Hutu while Tutsi power greatly increased. (p. 255)

The social stratification that was prevalent in traditional Rwanda is a reference to Bhabha's fixed spaces where the two essential groups occupy. The dominant group, which condescendingly regards the marginal group gloats in a vain superiority to cause disharmony in society. Using the divide and rule policy like the British in Kenya, the Belgians reinforced the duality with cash economy. It would be absurd to assume that the Tutsi-Hutu rivalry was purely economic given that before the advent of cash economy, the culture elevated the Tutsi to the highest stave. The colonialists simply returned to the past ways of life of the Rwandese people and reinforced it. It is no wonder Bhabha warns cosmopolitan societies against such tendencies as they would polarize their communities and cause political animosity. The struggle for independence in Rwanda was the struggle of the relegated Hutu against the oppressive Tutsi despots and their Belgian Big brothers. Goehrung R. (2017) writes:

Permeable social class boundaries of the pre-colonial times were institutionalized and racialized first by colonial authorities and then under the government of Habyarimana. The 1959-61 Hutu revolution was fought along ethnic lines to dethrone Tutsi privileged class... it established the relationship between ethnicity and power as a foundation of independent Rwanda and cemented the antagonistic notion that one group is in a position of authority excludes the Other. (p. 81)

In Bhabha's perspective, Juvenal Habyarimana, the first president of Rwanda, would have broken away from the tradition of cultural fixity or essentialism and opted for a third space to encourage cultural exchanges between the Hutu, Tutsi and Twa. Using a national language, like Nyerere, Habyarimana would have encouraged brotherhood to metamorphose the cultural diversity to a united nation state. Bhabha observes that the leaders of the independence movement are the torch bearers of hybridity, which enhances the creation of national culture and character in the cosmopolitan Africa. On the contrary, most independence leaders took the path of cultural essentialism by elevating the culture of their ethnic communities to create many nations in one. Habyarimana elevated the Hutu majority and excluded the Tutsi as a retaliatory measure. The aforementioned mess is based on the essentialist delusion that either Hutu or Tutsi is superior to the other owing to the tendency to return to past cultures. Ethnicity was thereby politicized and the death of Habyarimana was just but a trigger to the Rwanda Genocide of 1994. The Hutu accused Tutsi of shooting down the plane and the nation plunged into chaos.

Hall (1990) defines cultural identities as temporary forms of identification within dialogues of history and culture (p. 394). For Hall, Africans need not glue themselves on a certain foundation of culture. He writes, "[c]ultural identity is not a fixed essence at all lying unchanged outside history and culture... it is not once-and for-all. It is not a fixed origin on which we can make some final and absolute Return", (p. 395). Hall questions Edward Brathwaite's yearning to recover a lost Africa because with the fluid nature of cultural identity, the original Africa is no longer there. To imagine that Africa is same is colluding with the West in the delusion that Africa is a timeless zone of primitive and unchanging past (p. 399). He contends that cultural identity is a process that keeps changing from state to state and given that history interrupted through slavery and colonialism, Caribbeans should ask themselves what they have become, instead of who they were.

Habyarimana and other independence leaders, in Hall's perpective, erred to return to precolonial traditions and colonial policies that polarised the African people. After colonialism, they would have realized that the cultural identity of their people had changed. They were no longer Hutu, Tutsi, Twa, but Rwandese with a new touch of western ways. The major question was what they had become instead of who they were and now had a responsibility to buid a united state rather than unearth superiority contests of pre and colonial times. Bhabha asserts that past traditions protected the people against negative colonial influences. Nonetheless, during the struggle for independence Algerians,"[d]estroyed continuities and constancies of the nationalist tradition. They are now free to negotiate and translate their national identities," (p. 9-23). During the struggle for independence in African nations, essentialist "continuities" of colonialism that nurtured tribalism by divide and rule; the essentialist "constancies" of the African traditions, which exposed African communities to binary existence: Kikuyu/Luo, Hutu/Tutsi, Somali/Bantu; were razed to the ground. Africans were free to build new nations by selection of beneficial values from the maze of cultures at their disposal. Nelson Mandela opted for Bhabha's perspective after his release in 1994. His vision for a Rainbow Nation is indirect reference to a hybrid nation with a mosaic of cultures, which resulted in reconciliation and peace. Bhabha (as cited from Ashcroft et al, 1995) notes that hybridity eludes the politics of polarity. He asserts that hybridity reduces "disharmony and hostility between minority and dominant group" (p. 209). In other words, it deals a blow to fixity (cultural essentialism) thereby reducing cultural tensions between the two groups. Hybridity makes this possible because the Self is closer to and learns the attributes of the Other and the Other is closer and understands the attributes of the Self. Bhabha observes that the "interweaving of elements of the colonizer and colonized challenges the validity of any essentialist cultural identity" (Meredith, 2). And by pursuing hybridity we elude the politics of polarity because we are better informed of the attributes of the other, which gives way for negotiation and diplomatic settlement of disputes. Rumours, suspicions and unfounded fears are dispelled when one essentialist group moves closer to the other. After years in the fight for freedom, Nelson Mandela only got it by resolving to close ranks with his colonialist persecuters and oppressors.

7:7 Radical Feminism and the African Experience

It will be more accurate to argue not in the context of a monolith (African feminism) but rather in context of a pluralism that captures the fluidity and dynamism of different cultural imperatives, historical forces and localized realities conditioning women's activism in Africa. (Nnaemeka, 1998, p. 5)

African feminist narratives present the African woman on the continent as the innocent victim of the cruel, oppressive patriarchal system. African culture as a whole in most of these narratives presumably gives men authority to violate ethical standards in their treatment of women: men are gods, above the law thereby given to their primordial instincts. They commit diverse acts of sexual perversion without retribution from society because the culture permits them to do so. As much as feminist writing attempts to subvert dominant male hegemonies, it is essential to interrogate the claims, which these narratives depict and the extent of representation by the authors. Their narratives paint a grim picture of African culture and readers wonder how primordial traditions of Africa can get. Men characters defile house helpers, rape girls in their neighbourhoods, have sex with animals and worst of all exhume corpses to have sex. The audience wonders if this is true of evils of patriarchy in African cultures. Feminist scholars argue that male writers conceal the true picture of the woman's position in literature. Mills S. (1995) contends that there is a male hegemony in both the treatment of women in society and characterization in literary works. With Jacques Lacan and Burton Deirdre, they formulate feminist stylistics to counter the image of women in literature. Garvey B. (2012) observes that the female sentence lacks in rationality and authority, one which is essentially emotive, as the writer simply pours out her feelings… in a painless and structureless way (p. 2463). The male sentence is however authoritative, assertive with element of control and choice. Could this be one reason why feminist narratives from Africa paint a grim picture of African men?

Do the views of African feminist writers represent the plight of all African women? Is every African man a male beast or, this is just a skewed belief "Under Western Eyes?" This subsection examines representation of men, women and African culture in African feminist writing. Using ideas of Gayatry Spivak and Chandra Mohanty the sub chapter interrogates the representation in Nawal El Saadawi's *God Dies by the Nile*, Tsitsi Ndagarembga *Nervous Conditions* and Margaret Ogola's *The River and the Source*.

7:6.1 Feminist Scholarship in Africa and Beyond

The last half of the twentieth century saw the proliferation of women's movements and feminism the world over. Women began agitating for their rights by civil society, which spilled over to literature. They complained of misrepresentation by male writers and started writing to restore the position and image of women. In both fiction and nonfiction works, feminist writers depict male bashing and gender stereotyping which confounds their masculine counterparts. They depict men as brutes, sexual perverts and lazy. Deckard (1975) writes:

> In Africa for example, women used to conduct almost all Agricultural production while the men limited themselves mostly to hunting and warfare. The advent of European colonialism ended the intertribal war activities of the men. Since African men appeared idle to the Europeans, they used every means to force them into farming. (p. 239)

African men are therefore creatures of no economic use to the society after the banning of perilous interethnic clashes and raiding of neighbouring communities. The women and children do all the weeding and harvesting on the farm as the men possibly search for beer to return in the evening and demand for sex. Crehan K. (1983) reiterates Decard's argument that men were only of use in the case of hunting and fishing; however in crop farming, women and children constituted the basic unit. Men only gained access to products of cultivation through their relationships to women (p. 59). Quoting Booserup, Leavitt (1971) observes that the occupations of African men in Africa were warfare, hunting and felling trees. When the colonizers banned intertribal warfare, the men seemed to be idle... "Men could be come far better farmers than women if they could abandon their customary laziness" (p. 287). It is important to note that most of these feminist scholars hail from the west and tend to ignore the heterogeneity of Africa. Some African writers took cue from western feminists and started writing to defend the position of women and give a grim picture of African men. In her interview with Ayinne R. (2004), the feminist writer Amma Darko says:

We have started writing from our point of view because for a while you were writing for us...if we are writing, there are some pain that will have to come out... and I think rather than take it as male bashing, you must take it as a means to better understand the womenfolk of Africa. You were always portraying us as all enduring, all giving mothers. But I don't want to be all enduring... all giving.

Mawuli Adjei suggests that Darko like other African female writers uses an "irrational sentence" to depict the gender question. Citing Mariama Ba, Zeynab Alkali, Buchi Emecheta, Ama Ata Aidoo and Celix Beyala, Adjei observes that feminist writers present a situation in which women are victims of physical and psychological violence and men the perpetrators of the same (p. 48). Darko for instance exhibits strong anti-patriarchal tendencies and reduces men both to worthless, irresponsible physically grotesque images, wicked husbands, drunkards, rapists, exploiters, predators, monsters, sexually depraved, perverse and evil (p. 49). Frank (1987) summarises the African feminist's theme: man is the enemy, the exploiter and oppressor (p. 14).

As the reality of feminism sinks in the African collective psyche, scholars have emerged with divergent perspectives. Using Chandra Mohanty's ideas, African scholars have questioned the western feminists' treatment of Africa as a homogeneous entity. Oyeronke (2003) contends that western feminists' reference to Africa as one place with same cultural beliefs is "intellectual indolence and imperialist arrogance" (p. 59). He asserts:

> Readers get the impression that Africa is homogeneous as the inhabitants of a beehive. No sociologist would regard Paris or

Toronto as a homogeneous entity and Toronto has only two million people. But Africa is "Africa" and it is said all Africans look the same [...] Reference to Africa as if the continent were a homogeneous village are clearly nonsense. (p. 51)

Oyeronke's main argument is that if men in a Zambian village were lazy then it would be absurd to generalize the attribute to all African men in the continent. So is the case with other vices like brutality, sex perversion and drunkenness. Western feminists strive as much as possible to eradicate context in representation of African culture. Nawal El Saadawi complains that when submitting *The Hidden Face of Eve* to Beacon Press for publication, the publisher deletes the long preface to do away with her ideas on context (Nnaemeka, 2005, p. 54).

Oyewumi (2005) contends that looking at gender via the assumption that women are oppressed universally does account for differences in history and culture in different communities in the world, and particularly Africa. She adds that feminist theory originated in the West where men and women are conceived and brought up in a binary opposition and cannot be exported to other cultures (P. 11). These African scholars go on to invent a balanced form of feminism: nego feminism. Nnaemeka (2004) defines it as a "No Ego" feminism; the kind that fights for the rights of women with respect for the strategies that the people of that community have (p. 57). Nnaemeka writes:

> In their enthusiasm, our sisters usurp our wars and fight them very badly. The arrogance that declares African women "problems" objectifies us and undercuts the agency necessary for forging true global sisterhood. African women are not problems to be solved. Like women everywhere, African women have problems. More

important, they have provided solutions to these problems. We are the only ones to set the agenda and anyone who wishes to participate in our struggle must do so in the context of our agenda. (p. 57)

Nnamaeka suggests that western skewed feminists fight the gender war badly by stereotyping African men as sex perverts, lazy, predatory and other vices mentioned in aforesaid female writers. They depict African women as weak, helpless, miserable and hopeless creatures, which is not the case. Nnaemeka concludes that it is a Western yearning to demonise African men in the pretext of saving African women. In this study, the researcher applies the ideas of Chandra Mohanty, Gayatri Spivak and other postcolonial scholars to interrogate the ideas of feminist writers who have possibly misrepresented African culture and men to the world.

7:7.2 Critique of Radical Feminism

Post-colonialism in its most recent definition is concerned with persons from groups outside the dominant groups and therefore places subaltern groups in a position to subvert the authority of those with hegemonic power (p. 686). Ashcroft notes that post-colonial theory entails migration, slavery, suppression, resistance, representation and influences to discourses to imperial Europe (2). In this chapter, we employ the ideas of Chandra Mohanty and Gayatri Spivak to interrogate domination of African culture by western feminism. The following concepts will be essential in the chapter:

7:7.2.1 Representation

Spivak G. C (1988) questions the notion of representation in postcolonial studies. Poststructuralists crown the intellectual as a transparent medium through which the voices of the oppressed can be represented (67-72). Spivak contends that the colonized subaltern subject is irretrievably heterogeneous. She asks, "[c]an this difference be articulated? And if so by whom?" (79-80). In other words, to what extent do African Feminist writers represent the heterogeneous African women in Africa? There are those who do not see African traditions as oppressive at all. Furthermore, African culture is diverse; not all African cultures are oppressive to women. For Spivak, a feminist writer may either misrepresent some African women or in the attempt to give them voice start silencing some women. An attempt to give the oppressed women a voice will silence those who like the culture. Spivak gives the British example who in an attempt to speak for oppressed widows by banning *Sati* rite ended up silencing the Hindu culture. Can African feminists avoid this? Is their representation plausible? Apparently, the subaltern cannot speak; therefore the intellectual remains a medium. The study will apply Spivak's notion of representation to interrogate feminists writers' concerns to determine their effectiveness.

7:6.2.2 Skewed Generalisations

In her seminal paper, "Under Western Eyes," Mohanty (1984) critiques hegemonic western feminisms. She rejects the universality of the theories of western feminists and categorisation of the third world woman as a monolithic subject. Mohanty feels that the assumption that third world women are a coherent group (ignoring social factors) is problematic. She adds that the model of men as oppressors is not a universal model. Mohanty is against the oversimplification of the complexities across culture and gender to a binary division. She comes up with the concept of discursive colonialism where first world women (subjects) try to explain third world women (objects) to create power hierarchies and cultural domination. Mohanty gives a less pessimistic approach than radical feminists by criticising texts which claim that women worldwide are oppressed by male dominance. Mohanty suggests that women gain experience to get cultural insight to understand their situations rather than rely on a false sense of sisterhood. She interrogates universalizations like women are sexual objects, commodities and others, which collapse without due consideration to the context and situation. Whereas a veil symbolises oppression in one area, it signifies allegience to other women in Iran.

7:7.2.3 The Female Sentence and Retaliation

In their attempt to deconstruct male stereotypes in literature, African feminist writers paint a negative picture of men. Ogola (1994) deliberately presents male characters in the negative light. In the character of Otieno, Ogola represents men as lustful. He marries four wives and treats them like sluts; shockingly, he admires his brother's wife, Akoko. He is arrogant because he wants to beat Akoko while the brother is absent. He inherits the chiefdom and grabs owour's wealth after the death of Owang' Sino. In the character of Mark Sigu, Awiti's husband, men are stereotyped. When Awiti leaves him at Nakuru, he falls in love with another girl. Ogola presents men as unfaithful. At school, the principal suspends Aoro for being careless but when the girls, Vera and Becky are in school they behave well. The writer stigmatizes boys as careless and indisciplined. When Aoro marries a Kikuyu girl, Awiti accepts her happily but Mark says that he should marry a Luo girl because Kikuyus love money. Ogola portrays men as ethnocentric. Whereas Wandia furthers her studies to phd level, Aoro is contended with a Bachelors; men are complacent.

All the prime movers that represent the four generations in Ogola (1994) are women: Akoko, Nyabera, Awiti and Wandia are women. Although the story begins at Chief Gogni's house where Akoko is born, the male character, Gogni is made to unconventionally appreciate the girl child contrary to his contemporaries and then dies as soon as he sells her at thirty head of cattle. Owour Kembo though humble and exemplary character dies very early. The writer deliberately eliminates Obura, Akoko's noble firstborn. He dies in the First World War and when Owang' Sino, the younger sibling, becomes chief; the writer eliminates him under unconvincing circumstances. He chokes while eating fish and dies. Okumu, Nyabera'a husband, is very poor and relies on his wife, Nyabera, for sustenance. Like Gogni and Owour, Okumu dies early and leaves a helpless family. Towards the end of the story, the baton of generation is handed to Wandia. The death motif in male characters is a deliberate ploy by the writer to imply that women, not men, can perpetuate family line. The widow motif from Akoko, Nyabera to Wandia's mother is an unreasonable attempt to erase the role of men in the society. Ogola kills exemplary male characters such as Owour Kembo, Obura and Owang' Sino for women to take their place and do the good and lets funny men like Otieno to live longer to besmirch men's repute.

In her novel *So Long A Letter,* Mariam Ba paints a grim picture of African culture and men. The burial rites, which are presided over by men, are very absurd. After the death of Moudou, Ramatolouye is supposed to sacrifice her possessions to the family in law. She gives up her personality and dignity and becomes a thing in the service of the man who had married her (p. 40). The man's family takes all financial contributions made at the funeral and the widow is left empty handed. Men remain the sole owners of the family property; Ramatolouye's husband Moudou Fall acquired his house after joint savings with her but the title deed bears only his name (p.10). Men are cowardly people who manifest their insecurity through denying women education. Moudou is determined to pay fifty thousand Francs to Binetou to "to establish his rule" (p. 10) because going to school will make her critical. Men call educated girls "scatter brained and devils" (p. 14).

Furthermore, the men are lustful because they are obsessed with marrying even at a very old age. The story of Moudou Fall's second marriage is queer. Binetou tells Daba, his firstborn that she has a sugar daddy who buys her expensive dresses. She tells Daba that the sugar daddy wants to marry her. Besides, the man offers her a villa, mecca for parents, a car, monthly allowance and jewels. Binetou's mother persuades her to get married. Later, the sugar daddy happens to be Daba's own father, Moudou (p. 37). Worse still, men use divorce to abuse women. Ramatoloulaye writes, "I counted the abandoned and divorced women of my generation whom I knew…I knew a few whose remaining beauty had been able to capture a worthy man," (40). The men divorce the women when they age. The men have extramarital affairs and their lewdness is confounding. Samba Diack, Jacqueline's husband spends time chasing slender Senegalese women after marriage (p. 42). Jacqueline discovers notes, cheque stubs, bills from restaurants and hotel rooms. Jacqueline suffers constant fits of depression as a consequence of her husband's infidelity. Some men are so keen on inheriting widows even before the widow heals form the bereavement. Tamsir appears to propose to Ramatoloulaye a few days after her husband's death. Accompanied with Mowdo and the Imam, Tamsir says, "[y]ou are my good luck…I prefer you to the other one," (58). Rama replies that she has a mind; she is not an object to be passed from hand to hand (p 58).

Ba suggests that men are beasts due to their inability to control their natural desires. She asserts that it is through self control, ability to reason, to choose... that the individual distinguishes himself from an animal (87).

7.7.3 The African man- Brute and Sexual Pervert

Saadawi (1985) and Dangarembga (1988) present the African man as the brute and pervert and suggest that he should be killed. "I was not sorry when my brother died," goes the first sentence in Tsitsi Dangarembga's *Nervous Conditions* (1988). Tambudzai, the heroin of the story is so tormented by the father's brutal favouritism for the brother that she rejoices when her brother dies.

When the story begins, the men are depicted as bosses to be served by women. Her brother Nnamo orders her to fetch his luggage (p. 10). Nnamo beats Netsai for refusing to fetch the luggage. Jeremiah, the heroine's father detests it when Tambudzai reads the newspaper because by so doing she would be emulating her brother to fill her mind with ideas that would alienate her from reality of feminine living (p.34). He brutally denies Tambudzai a place in school. He asks, "Can you cook books and feed them to your husband? Stay at home with your mother. Learn to cook and be clean. Grow vegetables," (p. 15). While the brother, Nnamo is taken to a mission school, Tambu is denied right to education. The gender othering makes her feel like "by product of inexorable natural process" (p. 40). Tambu is ill provided for; whereas the brother has many clothes and exposed to the world at their uncle's home, Tambu wears the underwear when she visits the uncle after the brother's death (76). At her uncle's house, Tambu has never seen the switch, biscuit, sieve and cake (p.134). Men's insensitivity is also evident when during the Chrismas ceremony men sleep in good rooms while the women sleep in the kitchen. A man refuses to sleep in "public places"- the living room (p. 134). Dangarembga depicts the worst cruelty in men when

Babamkuru, Tambdzai's uncle gives her fifteen strokes of the cane for refusing to attend an uncle's wedding. She has to be obedient because she is a girl (p.174).

Tambu's behaviour is a sign of independence of mind which is a preserve of men. A woman has no mind of her own. Tambu's mother's mind belonged first to her father and then to her husband; it had not been hers to make up (p.155). Girls who are assertive are insolent and disrespectful. When Nyasha, Babamukuru's daughter, defends herself, Sigauke warns her not to talk. African tradition suggests that women should always be quiet (p. 115). Babamukuru is so infuriated because Nyasha has answered back. Babamukuru hits her, spits in her face and curses, "[s]he is not my daughter" (p. 116). He is also furious because Nyasha wears a short skirt and goes out to dance. Such dressing to him is ungodly. Nyasha's mother asks him whether he is proud of Nyasha. Not so; Babamukuru disapproves of that kind of dressing. Nyasha finds African culture queer; she says, "[t]hey control everything you do" (119) and adds that she was comfortable in England. Custom compels girls to kneel before elder men. At one point, Tambudzai having knelt several times in font of a disclaiming uncle grows tired and lets some water slipout (p. 41). There are many other instances that paint a grim picture of African culture in Dangarembgwa attempt to castigate patriarchy in African societies.

Saadawi (1985), *God Dies by the Nile* also attacks male dominance by presenting African men as callous sex perverts. The Mayor who is the major male character smiles unusually when a beautiful girl is mentioned. He tells Haj Ismail, "[t]he youngest is always tasty," (p. 12). Lust overwhelms him when he looks at Zeinab. Narrator says, "[h]e could see her firm rounded buttocks pressing up against the long *gabaleya* from behind," (p. 18). Sheikh Zahran says that she has a strange taste where women are concerned. 'Once he sets his eyes on a woman, he must have her; come what may', (p. 70). He is a rapist and this how he rapes Zeinab:

> His hands were now sliding on her thighs to her belly as he tried to lift her garment higher. But it was wet and stuck to her flesh. He pulled on it so hard that it split with rending sound. And he tore the remaining fold from around her body. (Saadawi, p. 64)

He kills Elwau after he flees with Neffisa, a girl with whom he had made love. He is even jealous when Hamzawi marries Fatheya, a beautiful girl. He schemes and arrests Galal for marrying Zeinab, a girl he had sex with. He has Hamzawi ruffled up for adopting a child claiming that he has brought evil on the land by adopting a bastard, Fatheya is killed while trying to save the baby: "Fatheya's clothes were torn away and her body shone white, and naked like that of a terrible mermaid in moonlit night," (145). There are several phallocentric symbols associated with the Mayor to signify his immorality: at the beginning the narrator says:

> He loved Cairo. The lamps shining on the dark surface of the tarmac roads. The coloured lights of the river side casinos reflected in the flowing waters of the Nile. The night clubs thronged with eating and drinking as they sat around the tables, the women dancing, their bodies moving, their perfume and soft laughter going through him. (p. 12)

The casino and night club represent sex, which he is obsessed with. The women dancing and bodies moving is the act of sex to him. The lamps represent his manhood and the flowing Nile waters, the female reproductive system. The image of the irongate associated with him is his manhood and roaring appetite for sex; the Mayor is fixated at the genitals.

Apart from the Mayor, sheikh Metwali is the most eccentric and sexually immoral in *God Dies by the Nile,* a man whose ID has trampled on the super ego in spite of his virtuous title. Like the Mayor, he is fixated at the genitals because he roams at night, exhume corpses to screw. He would exhume corpses:

> And if it was that of a female, he would crawl over it until his face was near the chin. If it was male, he turned it over on its face then crawled over it until the lower part of its belly pressed down on the buttocks from behind. (p. 74)

These sexual perversions are manifestation of the wicked instincts in his unconscious mind. His death instincts manifest in the way he seeks his bed among the dead. The writer says, "[h]e lived among the dead year by year," (p. 73). Women who met him would ask for a blessing. He would stretch out his hand and squeeze any part of their body he wished as saliva flowed down his beard (72). Metwali fondles the women he claims to be blessing. There is displacement in this because he cannot have sex with these women by virtue of his status as sheikh, he opts to bless them but in reality, he fondles them to derive sexual pleasure.

Sheikh Hamzawi is the cleric in Kafr El Teen Mosque. He is a close ally to the Mayor but he arranges for his murder because Hamzawi has a beautiful wife, Fatheya. Although the Mayor claims that Hamzawi is punished for picking an abandoned baby, which is bad omen, the truth is that Fatheya is beautiful and the Mayor wants her to slake his lust for sex. Sheikh Hamzawi stands out as a brute. He is quite aggressive towards the opposite sex in spite of his impotence. He admires Fatheya and compels her to marry him against her will.

Surprisingly, he does not have the potence to break Fatheya's virginity. The traditionist, Om Saber, is invited to break her virginity. The writer observes, "Fatheya felt the burning pain left by the woman's finger as it probed up between her thighs looking for blood," (41). Hamzawi's brutality is evident when he advises Haj Ismail and Masoud to beat the bride, Fatheya, to force her into marrying Sheikh Hamzawi (p. 40). He also loses temper and hits the adopted child.

Kafrawi is Zakeya's son and father to Neffisa and Zeinab, beautiful girls who the Mayor has designs on. Nefissa rejects the Mayor's advances and marries Elwau who is murdered by the Mayor out of jealousy. The Mayor demands for Zainab to serve him in his house but Kafrawi objects because he needs her for daily chores. Kafrawi is arrested, which infuriates Zakeya bitterly.

Kafrawi is portrayed as a sexual pervert, for example, the act of suckling the buffalo is phallocentric in itself. It resembles the act of sex and he goes further to have sex with his buffalo, Aziza (p. 61). The narrator says, '[t]he penis slid up into the inner warmth and was lost in great stillness, like an eternity, like death," (p. 61). His perverted nature is evident while playing with his daughter, Naffisa; they play around in a phallocentric manner, "[h]er small hand would play with his whiskers. He opened his mouth, closed his lips over her smooth fingers." This signifies sexual perversion in him.

Kafrawi's dreams depict the sexual perversion. In his dreams, he sees the dead body of his mother lying on the ground, which turns into the body of Elwau, the dead son-in-law. The sex instinct in this dream comes in form of Freud's Electra complex, where boys are sexually attracted to their mothers and change to learn their sex roles due to the fear for their fathers. The main phallocentric symbol associated with Sheikh Hamzawi is the female buffalo- Aziza. According to Sigmund Freud, Sexual perversion is as a result of fixation during early stages of development. Kafrawi is fixated on sex hence the bestiality in his personality.

Finally, Elwau is the young man who loves Neffisa, Kafrawi's daughter and flees away with her to the Mayor's infuriation. The Mayor pursues and kills him. Elwau is a sex pervert because he recalls how his cousin Yousef sodomised him, "Yousef caught him in an iron grip holding him by the back of his neck, threw him to the ground face downwards and wrenched his *galabeya* up his buttocks. He felt the powerful, heavy body press down on him…" (p. 66). It is evident that men characters in Saadawi (1985) commit unspeakable acts of sexual perversion against women, fellow men and animals.

7:7.4 Context, Representation and Interpretation in African Feminist Writing

Mohanty (1984) cross questions the skewed generalisations by Western feminists and treatment of African women as a monolithic subject. El Saadawi, Ba M., Dangarembga and Ogola use Western radical feminism to castigate the African man and African culture. In her perspective, all African women do not feel oppressed like Zakeya, Zeinab and Fatheya in Saadawi (1985) neither are they oppressed like Tambudzai and Nyasha in Dangarembga (1988). Ramatoulaye's experience in *So Long a Letter* is not every woman's experience in Africa. It is also interesting to note that some women embrace the culture and do not find their men brutal and perverted. Ramaoutalaye's lady mother-in-law and Binatou have embraced polygamy (p.7) and Ba blames them for Rama's problems. As much as feminist writers condemn polygamy, Mohanty suggests that the reader ought to understand the role of polygamy in the Islamic context to reach a reasonable interpretation. The woman Om Saber in Saadawi

(1985) loves African culture and embraces it with pleasure. She does not feel oppressed by the culture. The narrator says of her:

> Going from house to house, helping women in labour, circumcising the girls, piercing holes in their ears. At weddings, she would paint the feet of girls and women with red henna...at night tear the virgin's haymen with her finger... she was busy solving the problems of girls and women: carrying out abortions with a stalk of *mouloukheya*, throttling the newborn baby if necessary (Saadawi, 1985a, p. 92).

Whereas Dangarembga condemns Babamukuru for rejecting Nyasha's scanty dressing, Mohanty refers us to the context. Ba answers Dangarembga complaint, "[t]rousers accentuate ample figure of the black woman and should be used sparingly" (76). Nyasha is not in England and she is not a white woman; whereas white women look smart in trousers, black girls look indecent in them because of their different figures; hence Babamukuru's rejection. Mohanty emphasizes the different interpretations given to the veil in the west and Iran. Similarly, whereas Tambudzai's kneeling is a sign of oppression in the western sense, in Tambu's community, it possibly is just a simple sign of respect; whereas female circumcision is women's oppression in the western sense, it is a simple rite of passage to the Kikuyu in Ngugi's *The River Between*. Those Africans with exposure to western culture such as Dangarembga, Saadawi and Ba apply foreign standards to African culture and dismiss it. In the character of Nyasha, Dangarembga asserts that life is better in England . It is this that Mohanty refers to as an attempt of first world women to explain third world women to create power hierarchies and cultural domination.

Saadawi's argument that presents African men as sexual perverts and brutes comes under Mohanty's scrutiny. She sees it as an oversimplification of complexities across culture. Daba's husband in Ba's *So Long a Letter* is neither a sexual pervert nor a brute. He shares household chores and declares that Daba is his wife but not a slave or servant (73). Owour Kembo in Ogola (1994) shows not a single sign of sexual perversion and brutality. The narrator says, "Owour treated his wife like a queen…" (47), "and added a scandal to all his sins by failing to ever lay a finger on his wife," (37). Why do some characters like chief Gogni in Ogola (1994) treat their wives lovingly? Why does he appreciate Akoko after his birth if at all the girl child is absolutely appreciated? Gogni says, "[a] home without daughters is like a spring without source," (11). As Mohanty asserts, individual and cultural differences play an essential role in gender issues in Africa. Attributing villainy, sexual perversion and brutality in men to past cultures in Africa is possible misinformation of the world. Ba turns to the past to instruct modern girls on the importance of sexual morals: "Mothers of yore taught chastity; their voice of authority condemned extramarital wanderings," (p. 87).

Similarly, Spivak doubts the writers' capability to represent the subaltern. The intellectuals, feminist writers in this context, stand out to represent the oppressed women. But how is it plausible given that the subaltern is heterogeneous? Africa is a mosaic of cultures; some are matriarchal and others patriarchal. Some communities view women as queens and others as servants. How credible is feminist writers' argument that African men are oppressors? What do they make of the legend of Wangu wa Makeri, a Kikuyu female chief under whose iron rule men were slaves of the women? Underlying this legend is the fear among Kikuyu men that given opportunity, women can lord over them.

Furthermore, not all women believe that African culture encourages men to be oppressive owing to the heterogeneity among them. Om Saber in Saadawi's *God Dies by the Nile* and Binetou and lady mother-in-law in Ba's *So Long a Letter* absolutely embrace the culture. Whereas Om Saber effects female circumcision, the latter appreciate polygamy and do not see it a men's ploy to belittle women. Spivak doubts the writers' capability to represent the subaltern. The intellectuals, feminist writers in this context, stand out to represent the oppressed women. But how is it plausible given that the subaltern is heterogeneous?

7:6.5 The Male Sentence: Rationality and Moderation

Camara Laye in his work *African Child* presents African culture that is contrary to feminist writers. It is evident from his novel that Africa is vast and not all communities belittle the position of women. He writes:

> In our country, the woman's role is one of fundamental independence... she has great personal pride...we despise only those who allow themselves to be despised. (58)

Laye (in this autobiography) observes that his father had absolute respect for his mother and her prominence is further intensified by the miraculous powers she possesses due to her dignity. Unlike Saadawi's society where women are passive participants in religious matters, Laye's society allows women to perform certain rituals. There is an episode of the lying horse where she decrees:

> If it be that from the day of my birth I had knowledge of no man until the day of my marriage; and if it be true true that from the day of my marriage I have had knowledge of no man except my lawful husband...then I command you horse to rise up. (59)

The horse rises up to Laye's amazement. Laye's mother also has innate ability to discern witchdoctors. She warns some that if they continue with their evil, she would expose them. Her totem is the crocodile and she therefore draws water from the river without fear of any harm by the crocodiles.

The feminists' argument that Male African writers relegate women to mundane roles, Laye gives her mother a supreme character as important as the narrator himself. When presiding over meals, she forbids the young Laye from gazing at older guests. Even after Laye's formal induction to manhood, which is a preserve of men, she exerts great influence over him. She enters his heart without any warning to check his female friends and send away any that she dislikes. This is unlike the Mayor's son, Tariq, in Saadawi's *God Dies by the Nile* who harasses female servants and is visiting a prostitute in town (p. 51) but the Mayor's wife is just helpless. Although it is the father who presides over meals in Laye's society, it is the mother's presence that is felt as she controls the conduct and etiquette throughout meal time. At the end of the novel, Laye's father is reduced to insignificance. She almost bows for the mother to permit Laye to leave for Paris:

"Have you told my mother yet?" I asked.
"No," he replied, "we'll go together and give her the news."
"You wouldn't like to tell her yourself?"
"By myself? No, my son […] even if both of us go, we'll be outnumbered." (p. 146)

Laye (1953) clearly proves that not all African communities and families relegate women. In his community, particularly, his family, the woman has a chance to assert herself, guide the moral of children, including sons and be consulted before major decisions are made. The notion that African women are problems to be solved is non existent in Laye's society. Even Laye's friends such as Fanta and Marie do not exhibit the negative image that female characters are supposedly assigned by male writers. Laye's father who should be given the most heroic depiction by Laye, the male writer, is weak and insignificant.

7.7.6 Conclusion

The author set out to interrogate the application of philosophy in Africa. Using the ideas of Edward Said, Frantz fanon and Homi Bhabha, it is evident that cultural essentialism has tattered the social fabric of many African societies. The essentialisation of the Other has resulted in politisation of ethnicity that threatens national cohesion in countries such as Kenya, Somalia, Rwanda and Nigeria. Hybridity stands out as the better option for creation of national culture in African nations as it gives them a chance to select the best values after destruction of "continuities" and "constancies" during the struggle for independence. Tanzania stands out as the model of hybrid African nation, whose founder rejected cultural essentialism and politicisation of ethnicity. Nations that opted for cultural essentialism such as Kenya and Rwanda have politised ethnicity and faced ethnic animosities that threaten their very existence. In the last section, the author has interrogated the length at which radical feminism should be applied to African societies. Nega feminism is the way to go since the western strand of feminism has irrational generalisations that will have a negative impact on Africa's social fabric.

REFERENCES

Adjei M. (2009). Male Bashing and Narrative Subjectivity in Amma Darko's First Three Novels. *Journal of Literary Studies*, 1: P. 47-60.

Appiah, A. K. (1992). *In my Father's House*. New York. Oxford UP.

Ashcroft B., Gareth G., Hellen T., (eds). (1995). *Postcolonial Studies Reader.* London: Routledge.

Ayinne, R. (2004). Emmerging Issues in Emma Darko's Novels: *Beyong the Horizon, the House Maid* and *Faceless.* Legon. University of Ghana.

Baubock, R., & Faist T., (eds). (2010). *Diaspora and Transnationalism: Concepts, Theories and Methods.* Amsterdam: Amsterdam UP.

Bhabha, H. (1988). The Commitment to Theory. New Formations, 5: 9-23.

Bhabha, H. (1994).*The Location of Culture.* London: Routledge.

Achebe, Chinua (1975). The African Writer and English Language. In *Morning Yet Creation on Creation Day.* Doubley: Anchor Press.

Chweya, L. (Ed.). (2002). *Electoral Politics in Kenya.* Nairobi: Claripress Limited.

Crehan K. (1983). Women in Development in North Western Zambia: From Produce to Housewife. *Review of African Political Economy,27*: p. 59.

Deckard B. (1975). *The Women's Movement.* New York. Harper and Row.

Frank K. (1987). Women Without Men: The Feminist Novel in Africa. In Durosimi et al (ed). *Women in African Literature Today.* Trenton. NJ: African World Press

Fraser, R (1976). *West African Poetry.* London, Cambridge University Press.

Garvey B. (2012). Feminist Stylistics: A Lexico-Grammatical Study of Female Sentence in Austen's Pride and prejudice and Hume- Sotomi's *the General's Wife. Theory and Practice in Language Studies2*: P. 2460-2470.

Halakhe B.A. (2013). Ethnic Violence, Elections and Atrocity Prevention in Kenya. Global Centre for the Responsibility to protect, 4

Hall, S. (1990). Cultural Identity and Diaspora. In Rutherford, J. (ed). *Identity, Culture,*
Jerman, H. (1997). *Between Five Lines: The Development of Ethnicity in Tanzania with Special Reference to the Western Bagamoyo District.*Uppsala: Nordiska Afrikainstituet
Imbuga F. (1989). *Burning of Rags.* Nairobi. EAEP.
K.L. Godwin (1964). *Undertanding African Poetry.* Nairobi. Heinman Educational Publishers.
Kiondo, A. S. (2001). Group Differences in Political Orientation: Ethnicity and Class. In S. S. Mushi, R. S. Mukandala, & M. L. Baregu (Eds.), *Tanzania's Political Culture: A Baseline Study.* Dar es Salaam: Department of Political Science and Public Administration, University of Dar es Salaam.
Laye C. (1953). *The African Child.* Conakry. Farrar, Straus & Giroux.
Levitt, R (1971). Woman in Other Cultures. InVivian G. & Barbara M. (eds). *Woman in Sexist Society.* New York. Back Books.
Meredith, P. (1998). Hybridity in the Third Space: Rethinking Bi-cultural Politics in Aotearoa/NewZealand. Paper presented at Te Oru Rangahau Maori Research and Development Conference, University of Waikato.
Mills S. (1995). *Feminist Stylistics.* London & New York: Routledge.
Dangarembga T. (1988). *Nervous Conditions.* London. Women's Press Ltd.
Taiwo O. (2003). Feminism and Africa: Reflections on the Poverty of Theory. In Oyeronke O. (Ed). *African Women and Feminism: Reflecting on the Politics of Sisterhood.* (p 45- 65). Trenton: Africa World Press.
Thiong'o, N. (186). *Decolonizing the Mind.* Nairobi. Heinemann Educational Publishers.
Nnamaeka (2004). Nego Feminism: Theorizing, Practicing and Pruning Africa's Way. *Signs* 29: p. 357-385

Nnaemeka O. (2005). Bringing African Women into the Classroom (p. 51-65). *African Gender Studies Reader.* New York. Palgrave.
Nyongesa A. (2016). *The Endless Battle.* Nairobi. Royallite Publishers.
Ogola M. (1994). *The River and the Source.* Nairobi. Focus Publishers Ltd.
Ogot, B. A. (2005). *History as Destiny and History as Knowledge: Being Reflections on the Problems of Historicity and Historiography.*Kisumu: Anyange Press Limited *Reference to the Western Bagamoyo District.* Uppsala: Nordiska Afrikainstituet.
Oyaro, K. (2008). Kenya: The Media is not Innocent: Interpress News Agency.
Tripp, A. M. (1999). The Political Mediation of Ethnic and Religious Diversity in Tanzania. In C. Young (Ed.), *The Accomodation of Cultural Diversity: Case Studies.* London: Macmillan Press Ldt.
Oyewumi O. (2004). *African Women and Feminism: Reflecting on the Politics of Sisterhood.* Trenton, NJ: Africa World Press.
Saadawi E. (1985). *God Dies by the Nile* .London. Zed Books.
Spivak, G. C. (1988). Can the Subaltern Speak? Marxism and Interpretation of Culture. In Carry N. & Lawrence G. (Eds). London: Macmillan, P. 66-104.
Ulli B. & Moore G. (1963). *Penguin Book of Modern African Poetry.* London. Penguin Group.

www.ingramcontent.com/pod-product-compliance
Lightning Source LLC
Chambersburg PA
CBHW011713290426
44113CB00019B/2661